The Denver Dry Goods

· WHERE COLORADO SHOPPED WITH CONFIDENCE ·

MARK A. BARNHOUSE

THE
History
PRESS

Published by The History Press
Charleston, SC
www.historypress.net

Copyright © 2017 by Mark Barnhouse
All rights reserved

Front cover: Author's collection.
Back cover, top left: Author's collection; *inset*: James J. O'Hagan collection.

First published 2017

Manufactured in the United States

ISBN 9781467135368

Library of Congress Control Number: 2016961491

To the memory of Horace Alfred Pratt, 1916–1975

CONTENTS

FOREWORD

*The Denver: a division of Associated Dry Goods Corporation,
one of the leading retail organizations in the United States with
fourteen major divisions throughout the country.
The Denver: "Where Denver Shops with Confidence."
The Denver: "Where Colorado Shops with Confidence."*

By the time we arrived in the mid-1970s, The Denver had been serving customers in the Rocky Mountain region for over eighty years. By building on its reputation for premier service, merchandise selection, quality and value, together with a philanthropic commitment to the well-being of the markets in which it operated, the company achieved record sales and profits during the decade that followed. It was an exciting time for us, bringing products from around the globe to a community rapidly growing in consumer sophistication.

We were fortunate enough to join The Denver Dry Goods Company at a turning point in its history. From the early 1970s, it began a rapid expansion along the Front Range. Full-line department stores were opened in Colorado Springs, Southglenn, Aurora, Englewood, Northglenn and Southwest Plaza. Full fashion stores opened in Fort Collins, Boulder, Pueblo and Billings, Montana. These new stores joined Downtown, Cherry Creek, Lakeside and Greeley.

The Denver quickly became the leading retail powerhouse and the upscale leader of quality fashion merchandise. The growth occurred because of its acceptance by a strong customer base, parent company

A 1930s–40s roadside billboard advertises the store "Where Colorado Shops with… Confidence." *Linda Lebsack collection.*

Associated Dry Goods' commitment to a constant, strong senior management group and the training and development of its people. All of this resulted in superior financial results and the backing of its corporate ownership.

A strong organization with highly developed and motivated employees who stayed with the company and grew with it fed the ability to have strong merchandising trends that were based on quality and fashion. These merchandising concepts were widely accepted by the consumer.

It is, however, our colleagues and associates who provide our most enduring memories. Their dedication to making it the store "where Denver shops with confidence" was the driving force for success. A history of The Denver that doesn't recognize the accomplishments of these outstanding men and women would be incomplete.

When it came time to say goodbye after ninety-one years because of a corporate buyout on the New York Stock Exchange, it was front-page news for many months on the *Denver Post* and the *Rocky Mountain News*. Thus, a strong institution of over three thousand employees committed to a culture of excellence was lost to the retail community and its customers forever.

Many thanks go to Mark Barnhouse for allowing us to be part of this history. There are still many of us who remember our years with The Denver with great fondness and pride. We are proud to have been a part of this exceptional enterprise.

F. Joseph Hayes and James J. O'Hagan

F. Joseph Hayes was the last president of The Denver Dry Goods Company, serving in that position from 1980 until 1987. He had previously served as assistant treasurer and as vice-president/chief financial officer. James J. O'Hagan was The Denver's last vice president of operations, serving from 1978 until 1987, after a career there that began in 1973.

ACKNOWLEDGEMENTS

The writing of a book is usually thought of as a solitary pursuit, but no author, including myself, could produce the history of a great department store such as this one without the help of many other people (listed here in roughly chronological order). I am indebted to "Dr. Colorado," Thomas J. Noel, who provided his usual sage advice, along with some fine photos from his collection. I am deeply thankful to Colorado's foremost dealer in western Americana, Linda Lebsack, for her timely discovery and sharing of a cache of documents and photographs related to The Denver Dry Goods Company. Two former Denver Dry Goods executives, F. Joseph Hayes and James J. O'Hagan, shared their memories and observations, which I greatly enjoyed and which informed the text. Thanks to Joe and Jim, too, for their wonderful contribution to this book in writing its foreword and to Jim for sharing his extensive collection of Denver Dry Goods memorabilia. Architectural historian Dr. Kathleen Corbett pointed me toward the works of Richard Longstreth, which have proved invaluable to my understanding of the ways department stores evolved over the twentieth century. Current residents Mark Bochnak and Richard Bruce gave me a tour of the Denver Dry Goods Building so that I could get a better understanding of its transformation into a residential/commercial adaptive reuse project that wonderfully preserves a Denver landmark. Bill Eloe kindly allowed me to use a very rare image from his collection of nineteenth-century western photography. As always, I thank the wonderful staffs of the Western History and Genealogy Department of the Denver Public Library, the Stephen H.

Hart Library of History Colorado (particularly photo research librarian Melissa Van Otterloo), the Colorado Railroad Museum (collections curator Stephanie Gilmore and volunteer Bill Brown) and the Special Collections department at the Auraria Library. As she has done for all of my previous books, Coi Drummond-Gehrig, digital image collection administrator of the Denver Public Library, located some wonderful photographs that I wasn't able to find myself, for which I am deeply grateful. Too numerous to name individually, I give collective thanks to the many vendors at the Denver Post Card Show and the Rocky Mountain Book and Paper Fair—these events are great resources for historians and for people who just love historical things. Finally, thanks go to my editor at The History Press, Artie Crisp, who provided helpful advice and encouragement throughout the process.

Introduction

THE END OF AN ERA

No one can claim to live in the civilized world if he doesn't have a big department store across the street from where he works. If I wanted to, I could walk over there in 45 seconds, buy a new suit, shirt, tie, socks and shoes, and be transformed into someone really important-looking almost as fast as Superman could get in and out of his phone booth. I've always told myself I'd do that silly trick someday when I had the money, and now it appears I've let another one of the downtown Denverite's delights slip through my fingers.[1]

WE'VE COME TO SAY GOODBYE

"The Denver to Close"—residents of the Mile High City woke up to this shocking *Denver Post* headline on Saturday, January 31, 1987, although most had heard the sad story on local television and radio news broadcasts the night before. The paper used its largest headline type, normally reserved for major events, such as wars and assassinations, to announce the previously unthinkable demise of a Colorado institution (and one of its largest advertisers). For the front-page photograph, the editors chose a poignant image of sixty-two-year-old housewares department employee Millie Krause wiping tears away after news broke. The *Post* had long maintained a close relationship with The Denver Dry Goods Company (simply "The Denver" in its last decades). It was not entirely coincidental when, seeking larger quarters after World War II, the paper chose to build its new plant diagonally across the intersection of Fifteenth and California Streets from

We've come to say goodbye.

We've been friends for such a long time — nearly a century. Growing up together in Colorado, we've shared your lives. You came to us to celebrate your triumphs, mark your milestones, solve your problems, help out in your emergencies. You depended on us to supply your daily needs, to bring you the best of the new, to inspire you with ideas, to fulfill your dreams.

We traveled the globe to lay the world at your feet. And above all, we put our heart into everything we did so that you would find The Denver a warm and friendly place to come to.

But nothing, dear friends, is forever. It's time, now, for others to take over; in May D&F we know we leave you in good hands. And what's more, on May 3 at May D&F Cherry Creek, Cinderella City, Northglenn and Aurora, you'll find many familiar faces from The Denver to serve you in the same old friendly way.

It's time to say farewell.

Remember us kindly.

the Denver

The Denver's advertising department prepared this farewell message to run in the *Denver Post* and *Rocky Mountain News*, but May Department Stores Company executives would not permit its publication, fearing customer backlash. *Jim O'Hagan collection.*

the store, simplifying the daily delivery of advertising materials (in that predigitized era, when such proximity was crucial). The *Post*'s archrival, the *Rocky Mountain News*, favored a similarly matter-of-fact (and equally devastating) headline that day: "May D&F consolidation to eliminate The Denver."

Most Coloradoans knew both stores well. May-D&F and The Denver were as much rivals as the two newspapers, and both claimed to be the dominant department store in Colorado. Their boastfulness ignored the popular Joslin's, a chain that bested both The Denver and May-D&F in sales; a notch below them in the unofficial hierarchy of Colorado stores, Joslin's was perceived as less elegant in both décor and image. May D&F, although created by a 1957 merger, was actually the older store, its predecessor, Daniels and Fisher, having been founded in 1864, just six years after Denver's birth. Parent company May Department Stores Company of St. Louis had deep Colorado roots as well. David May founded what would become a national chain when he opened a store in a wood-framed canvas tent in booming Leadville in 1877, selling "Levi's and longies" (red woolen underwear) to silver prospectors and fancy ball gowns to their ladies after the jackpots rolled in. By contrast, The Denver Dry Goods Company was a relative newcomer, birthed in 1894, after the city for which it was named had already become a major regional metropolis.

The news of The Denver's closure hit the city hard, seemingly yet another nail in its coffin. How different the mood was in early 1987 from what it had been a decade or so earlier, when the city was enjoying the greatest boom in its history. Seemingly every other week in the late 1970s and early 1980s brought news of a new downtown skyscraper here or a new shopping mall there. Denver was being transformed, thanks in large part to a spike in oil prices; boosters called the city the "Houston of the north," with major new buildings named for energy producers like Amoco and ARCO and speculative office buildings filling up with satellite offices of *Fortune* 500 companies. The arts flourished, too, with the opening of a new performing arts complex and a new history museum, and high rates of philanthropic giving (as a matter of course, both The Denver and May-D&F were frequent donors). The beloved Denver Broncos ("the Orange Crush") even went to the Super Bowl for the first time in January 1978. It did not matter that they lost that game; the point was that Denver was finally a "major league city," in many senses of the term.

Then, as had occurred repeatedly over the city's history, Denver's economy, too dependent on one extractive industry (gold or silver in the nineteenth century, oil in the twentieth), crashed when the price of crude fell. Building projects were canceled and recent arrivals began leaving. Longtime Denverites assumed the city would eventually come back, as it always had done, with its institutions mostly intact. It was only necessary to ride it out, and in fact, Denver would do just that, investing public money on a series of projects (a new convention center, a central library and an airport) that kept the metropolitan economy afloat when private industry struggled.

One institution would not remain intact, however: the city's beloved eponymous department store, The Denver. Completely unrelated to Colorado's boom-and-bust cycle, the department store industry was undergoing a national transformation as it struggled to keep consumers from shifting more and more of their spending toward a new type of retailer born in the 1960s that by the 1980s had become the default choice for many budget-conscious households: the discount superstore, as exemplified by Walmart, Target and Kmart. Some of this shift was driven also by a multi-decade wage stagnation that effectively shrank the potential market for department stores. To combat these threats, executives looked for ways to "scale up," growing larger through mergers and buyouts. May Department Stores Company, already one of the nation's leading operators, was one of the biggest buyers of other chains, and in August 1986, it reached an agreement with Associated Dry Goods of New York City, parent of The Denver, as well as Lord & Taylor (New York), J.W. Robinson's (Los Angeles) and nearly a dozen other regional names, on terms of a buyout.

When the merger news broke, May announced to Colorado shoppers (and indirectly, political leaders) that both May-D&F and The Denver stores would remain in operation and continue to compete with each other as they always had done. The new owner gave hints that The Denver might be repositioned as the more upscale of the two chains, creating a clear differentiation, leaving May-D&F to more directly compete with rival Joslin's for the broad middle of the market; this notion was amplified by newspaper articles quoting retail analysts, most of whom thought shifting The Denver's merchandise mix in a more designer-oriented direction would make sense. Perhaps May executives were sincere in making these projections, and Colorado's weakened economy prevented them from making good on them. Or perhaps they were just trying to ensure the Federal Trade Commission, charged with protecting consumers from higher prices brought about by reduced competition, would not try to prevent the merger or force them to sell The Denver to a rival. Whatever May's motive may have been, the news of The Denver's closure after more than nine decades hit the city hard.

The Heart of Denver

This book is not a sad story, but it does have an unhappy ending, which is why it begins with the end in this introduction—so the reader will not dread it later. The tale begins with pioneer merchants coming west seeking their fortunes, makes a brief detour through insolvency and then rolls on for decades, through most of the twentieth century. During that time, successive generations of Denverites boarded streetcars, drove carriages, rode buses or steered automobiles to Sixteenth and California Streets, which intersection, thanks to The Denver Dry Goods, became the busiest corner on Denver's main shopping street. In many ways, Sixteenth and California, and the store itself, embodied the "heart" of Denver, much more than the elegant Civic Center flanked by the state capitol and the City and County Building, the magnificent Municipal Auditorium, the vast City Park or any other facility built by the citizens to beautify their city. Those were ornaments, nice to visit on occasion or show off to out-of-town relatives, but The Denver Dry Goods was part of their daily lives.

The store had rivals for Denverites' affection, of course. The chief of these was Daniels and Fisher, running a full block along Sixteenth between Lawrence and Arapahoe Streets and boasting, in its magnificent twenty-one-story tower, the tallest building between Chicago and the West Coast when it was built. Until 1958, when the First National Bank overtook it in height, it was the most prominent element on Denver's skyline. But as beloved as that store was, over time it lost steam, thanks partly to its location in "lower" downtown, an area that gradually became seedy, more run-down with each passing decade. In its early decades, Daniels and Fisher was the nucleus of Denver shopping, with near neighbors the May Company, the Golden Eagle and Appel and Company providing a reason to patronize that section of Sixteenth Street. Momentum began to shift, however, when, in 1905, May moved uptown to Champa Street, halfway between the two powerhouses Daniels and Fisher and The Denver Dry Goods, and over the course of subsequent decades, central Sixteenth Street, anchored by The Denver, became the main draw.

McNamara Dry Goods Company (The Denver's predecessor, the story of which is told in chapters 1 and 2) found itself in a largely residential area when it moved to Sixteenth and California Streets in 1889, with wags joking that it was "out in the country." By the early 1900s, however, it was clear to the city's smaller and younger merchants that its siting, so far from the city's once-dominant retail zone at Larimer and Lawrence Streets, had been a visionary move. The vast and growing Denver Dry Goods exerted a gravitational pull, like Jupiter on its many moons, and it was soon joined by Merritt W. Gano and Company (later partnered with William D. Downs, as Gano-Downs), A.T. Lewis and Son, the Neusteter Company (an important rival to The Denver Dry Goods for the trade of the city's upper crust), menswear purveyor Cottrell's, shoe store Fontius, stationery and bookseller Kendrick and Bellamy and many others in this newly fashionable section of Sixteenth Street. Even as late as the early 1950s, when national chain J.C. Penney and Company wanted to plant a new six-story Colorado flagship, it chose the corner diagonally opposite The Denver Dry Goods, because trade at The Denver was brisk and it hoped to garner some of that traffic.

A trip to The Denver was a special occasion. Neighborhood shops might be fine for mundane purchases like socks or underwear, but when a new Easter suit, a new set of "best" china or a fancy dress to wear to a daughter's wedding was required, Sixteenth and California would beckon. Upon entering, the shopper was greeted with what the store claimed was the "longest department store aisle in America," running four hundred feet from the Sixteenth Street door, past glass counters full of perfumes and cosmetics, past banks of elevators, under the store's famous clock, all the way to another door at Fifteenth Street. The store's tone, while busy, was dignified; instead of a loudspeaker, a system of bells alerted employees to where they were needed. Shoppers may never have quite grasped what the bells signified, but store staff, following strict codes for dress and behavior, certainly did. Patrons, too, took their dignity seriously, with suits and hats (often Stetsons, sold by the store in great volume) for men and white gloves worn by women and girls. Throughout the store, floor upon floor, were departments for every sort of item imaginable, from books and stationery to expensive furs; from notions and fabrics to formalwear; from the smallest spoon to the largest dining room suite; and from cowboy suits for the junior *Davy Crockett* fan to actual saddles, tack and other items used by real working cowboys. The Denver had it all, and in the basement, nearly every department was replicated with budget pricing.

When it was all too overwhelming, when shoppers just couldn't try on another dress, they could always head upstairs to an institution inside an institution: The Denver's Tea Room. Located after 1924 on the fifth floor, the tearoom was both a refuge and a place to see and be seen. It became such an integral part of downtown Denver that on most days, the majority of its two thousand or so diners weren't shopping at all but had come to the store for the express purpose of having lunch and greeting people (what

Crowds lined up for one last lunch in the Tea Room during the store's final days. *Denver Public Library, Western History Collection.*

today would be called "networking"). The Denver even had a special express elevator to the tearoom, so the city's movers and shakers wouldn't have to stop at each floor on their way up or down. When the store finally closed, people were arguably more upset by the loss of the tearoom than by the store itself, judging by articles written at the time and from the memories of former patrons.

The Denver was unique among major American department stores for bearing the name of its city. While the nineteenth-century western urban landscape was dotted with shops that called to mind great cities (a "New York Store," a "Boston Store" or a "City of Paris"), if there was ever a "Chicago Dry Goods Company" or an "Atlanta Dry Goods Company," they did not survive. Instead, those cities had Marshall Field and Company and Rich's, just as Denver had Daniels and Fisher and Joslin's. But Denver also had *The* Denver, a store that proudly wore the name of the largest city in nearly a one-thousand-mile radius. Named for the metropolis, it was the city's beating heart. But it didn't begin its 110-year journey as "The Denver."

1

AN IRISH MERCHANT

When the visitor to Niagara first gazes upon this stupendous waterfall, the mind fails to grasp the sublimity and grandeur of the scene before him....A somewhat similar feeling is experienced when one first enters the mammoth dry good emporium of M.J. McNamara, corner [of] *Fifteenth and Larimer.*[2]

PIONEER MERCHANTS

Arriving in 1870, Michael J. McNamara was by no means the first man to come to young Denver with the idea of making his fortune as a merchant prince, but he may have been one of the more colorful ones to do so. When his store, McNamara Dry Goods Company, was in its heyday in the late 1880s and early 1890s, he would personally greet important customers arriving by carriage. McNamara was "genial, a wit, a dandy in a broadcloth Prince Albert wing collar with opulent Prince de Joinville tie, lilac colored waistcoat, gray striped trousers creased to a razor's edge, needlepoint and patent leather shoes." With his extraverted personality, he had many friends (who called him "Mack"), and he was part of nearly every important civic betterment committee. His was a classic Irish American success story, although at the end of his life, he would be remembered more for his generosity and geniality than for his fortune or business acumen.[3]

Born in Carrick-on-Shannon, County Leitrim, Ireland, in 1843, McNamara, along with his family, made the arduous trek across the Atlantic in 1849 during the height of the Irish potato famine; they landed in Philadelphia. Six years later, at the tender age of twelve, McNamara went to work for a linen importer, a job he kept until he was eighteen. Looking for brighter opportunities, he moved to St. Louis, where he worked for another dry goods house, Ubsdell, Pierson and Company (one of a number of predecessors to that city's Famous-Barr department store) for five years. The Gateway City was so well established by this time that if a man wanted to go into business for himself, he faced stiff competition. Sensing greener pastures at the western end of Missouri, McNamara opened a short-lived store in the town of Liberty, near Kansas City. Finally, in 1870, he came to Denver, the city he would call home for the rest of his life.[4]

Michael J. McNamara, an Irish merchant, a wit and a dandy. *History Colorado Collection.*

The infant prairie metropolis of Denver was certainly an interesting place in 1870, but it was not yet apparent that it would grow into a major American city. After its founding in 1858, Denver, which merged with nearby rival Auraria in 1860, stagnated for a decade. The 1860 census counted 4,749 souls. The population had grown by a scant 10 people, to 4,759, when the decennial count was taken in 1870, reflecting a long period of inertia after the initial boom. The 1860s had seen an exodus of its southern citizens after the outbreak of the Civil War, gone home to don the gray uniforms of the Rebels. The infamous Sand Creek Massacre of 1864—when a Colorado Territory militia force of 700 Denver men led by Colonel John P. Chivington, under the orders of territorial governor John Evans, surprise-attacked a peaceful village of Cheyenne and Arapaho people and killed over 160 of them (the majority women and children)—gave the town and territory a reputation for violence that shamed its kindlier citizens. Finally, Denver boosters had to suffer the humiliation of seeing the transcontinental railroad bypass Colorado entirely when the Union Pacific chose an easier route through southern Wyoming in 1867. Cheyenne, established by the railroad as a base of operations, seemed poised to become the most important city in this part of the West. Denver's future was saved by the arrival in 1870 of not one but three railroads that connected the town to the nation's rail system: the Denver Pacific, the Kansas Pacific and the Colorado Central, all established by Colorado people in an effort not to be left behind. The boom was back on, just in time for McNamara.[5]

By 1873, when noted English traveler Isabella Bird visited, Denver was already growing fast, although she, having traveled through much of the world, could recognize braggadocio when she saw it:

> From a considerable height I looked down upon the great "City of the Plains," the metropolis of the Territories. There the great braggart city lay spread out, brown and treeless, upon the brown and treeless plain, which seemed to nourish nothing but wormwood and the Spanish bayonet. The shallow Platte, shriveled into a narrow stream with a shingly bed six times too large for it, and fringed by shriveled cotton-wood, wound along by Denver, and two miles up its course I saw a great sandstorm, which in a few minutes covered the city, blotting it out with a dense, brown cloud.

But Bird recognized that the city was no longer a raw frontier town, that it was now "a busy place, the *entrepôt* and distributing point for an immense district, with good shops, some factories, fair hotels, and the usual deformities and refinements of civilization. Peltry shops abound, and sportsman, hunter, miner, teamster, emigrant, can be completely rigged out at fifty different stores." This was fertile territory for anyone wanting to make his fortune in the retail trade.[6]

It is likely that McNamara's Liberty, Missouri venture was not successful, because he did not immediately attempt to open his own store in Denver after his arrival. Instead, he became a clerk at a now-forgotten concern (but one that was a leading store in its day), Brooks, Giddings and Company, a Larimer Street shop.[7] There, he met another clerk, Edgar H. Drew. Born in Lowell, Massachusetts, Drew had been too young to join as a regular soldier at the 1861 outbreak of the Civil War but followed his father into the army nonetheless, serving as the regimental drummer boy. The year 1864 found Drew in Boston, where he worked as a clerk in a wholesale dry goods establishment, remaining there until 1868. He then moved to New York City, continuing to work in wholesale dry goods but left that city for Lowell, Massachusetts, in 1875. Like McNamara, he decided that he would find better opportunities out west, so in 1877, he came to Denver.

With Colorado's economy beginning to boom thanks to silver strikes at Leadville, people were flocking to the state that year. (David May, another pioneer merchant whose firm will become important to this story in the final chapter, was one of those 1877 migrants, opening a store in Leadville itself.) Drew and McNamara decided the time was right to strike out on their own and so became partners in a new venture, Drew and McNamara & Company. Needing a home for their new business, they soon settled on the busy southern corner of Fifteenth and Larimer Streets. This had been the site of the very first log cabin in Denver, erected in late 1858, the year of the city's birth, by Denver city founder General William H. Larimer and his son. In 1859, pioneer merchants (and brothers) George Washington Clayton and William M. Clayton erected a one-story building in front of this cabin for their store and a few years later replaced it, along with Larimer's cabin, with a two-story brick edifice in which they established an emporium that sold groceries, dry goods and miners' equipment. Dusty (and frequently muddy) Larimer Street may have still been unpaved, but a board sidewalk in front meant that dirt wouldn't follow customers inside.[8] It was this structure that Drew and McNamara leased for their fledgling venture. They weren't aware that their shop would one day become The Denver Dry Goods Company, but it was fitting that a store with such a name could trace its roots to the very spot where the city's founder had once lived (in the twentieth century, The Denver's publicity department made the most of this fact, calling it the "first of many firsts" associated with the store).[9]

Drew & McNamara was an immediate hit because it was the partners' democratic business philosophy to cater to all classes; the store was "filled with goods of every grade from the finest to the cheapest." Drew frequently traveled to New York to buy stock, leaving McNamara to attend to the store in Denver. Thanks to Drew's efforts, customers could expect the "latest Parisian novelties" and "fine Hamburg embroideries" in a western frontier city two thousand miles removed from America's Atlantic seaports. One account, probably exaggerated but maybe not, claimed that the wife of an Ohio senator, upon visiting Denver, saw "more fine goods in Denver than in Cincinnati," thanks to her visit to Drew and McNamara.[10]

In 1880, three years after setting up together, for reasons unknown Drew wanted out of the business, so McNamara bought his share and removed Drew's name, calling the store simply M.J. McNamara & Company. He soon took on a junior partner, Leonard H. Flanders, another Brooks, Giddings veteran, whose name would not appear in the firm's name. (In 1886, when he reorganized as the McNamara Dry Goods Company, Flanders and George W. Clayton would both be listed as board members, although Flanders would later establish his own firm, Flanders Dry Goods.) Soon, the

Drew & McNamara's store on Fifteenth and Larimer Streets (*left*), in a building erected in the 1860s by George Washington Clayton on the site of General William Larimer's log cabin; circa 1877. Today, this block is Larimer Square. *Bill Eloe collection, stereoview photograph by William Gunnison Chamberlain.*

ambitious McNamara was getting noticed, finding customers and making friends. By April, less than a month after the dissolution of his partnership with Drew, the "popular store of M.J. McNamara" was "attracting much attention" for its "magnificent line of ladies' muslin underwear" and its "lovely styles of parasols and sun umbrellas, at prices astonishingly low."

Just a few months later, the busy month of July convinced McNamara that his original premises were too small for his dreams and his growing throngs of customers, so he leased the adjacent shop (in a separate building next door), previously occupied by a firm called Monk and Stapper, and knocked openings through the wall. In this doubled space, he could now accommodate even more "elegant line[s] of dress goods, dress trimmings, cloaks, dolmans, ulsters, shawls, lades, embroideries, handkerchiefs, gloves, hosiery, notions, &c., &c.," along with "muslin underwear, merino underwear, &c., and also table linen, towels, napkins, quilts, comforts and blankets" and a "fine line of cloths and cassimeres, repellants and ladies cloths, flannels &c." By the first day of 1881, his business had "more than doubled," his "wholesale trade extend[ed] all over the west," and his store was becoming known as the place where Denver shoppers could find what they required to keep pace with the fashions of New York City.[11]

To understand how McNamara's establishment differed from the general store associated with the frontier west in the nineteenth century (such as those of the Clayton brothers or Monk and Stapper in the same premises) and why his contemporaries found it marvelous that he would stock such an impressive selection in what was still almost a frontier town, some context might be helpful. The department store idea obviously did not originate with McNamara but had developed over the course of the nineteenth century from precedents set by retailers in Paris and London. Alexander Turney Stewart (better known as A.T. Stewart and, like McNamara, an Irishman) is generally considered the father of the American department store. His 1848 "Marble Palace" at 280 Broadway in New York City—followed by his 1862 "Iron Palace," occupying nearly a full block on Broadway at Tenth Street—set the precedent and scale future retailers would follow. One of these was Chicago's Marshall Field, who made his reputation and a vast fortune through fine customer service, instructing his employees to follow his famous dictum "give the lady what she wants."

These vast new emporia by Stewart, Field and others catered to, and were the product of, a new kind of clientele: the American woman with some money to spend and enough leisure time in which to do it. In the middle of the nineteenth century, she emerged in large cities as "the director of family consumption," and she gravitated toward the new department stores as "relief from the boredom of familial confinement or the drudgery of domestic routine," per historian Gunther Barth. The new retail palaces, organized into departments, contrasted with "the orderly confusion of the general store and the exclusive air of the specialty shop where gloves or shawls waited in boxes for the right customer to call." Department stores catered not just to the most affluent but also to women of more modest means, and the clearly marked, pre-set prices (required when an institution like A.T. Stewart employed as many as two thousand people) allowed these customers to browse without the embarrassment of having to ask about cost. With so many women coming to downtown areas on their own or in group shopping excursions, a formerly all-male environment evolved into something more civilized, and the elegant new store buildings "introduced into the downtown section the same sense of spatial order that the department store had brought to large-scale retailing." Ultimately, said Barth,

> with its far-ranging utility, the department store reflected the culture of the modern city. It constantly assessed people's hopes for a better life and responded to their dreams. As a creative social force, the department store sustained the shared experience of shopping, produced a new form of communal life, and provided links among heterogeneous people. Ultimately, the department store gave urban life a downtown focus, not only bestowing charm and civility but also evoking democratic qualities that enriched the urbanity of the modern city and reaffirmed its egalitarian nature.[12]

In establishing the future Denver Dry Goods Company, McNamara was following the lead of eastern merchant princes and helping civilize what had been a raw frontier community only two decades previously.

A GRAND NEW EMPORIUM

Denver was growing rapidly in the booming 1880s, and the two-story 1860s brick building erected by the Clayton brothers and leased by McNamara at Fifteenth and Larimer Streets was beginning to look dowdy and old fashioned. The civic-minded Claytons were never ones to stand still (William had been Denver's mayor in 1868–69), so they determined to bring their Fifteenth and Larimer property up to date by pulling down the two-story brick building and erecting in its place a magnificent new four-story palace; Michael J. McNamara would occupy the entire building with his thriving store, a veritable A.T. Stewart in miniature. The Clayton Block, as it was originally known (today it anchors the popular Larimer Square shopping and dining block and is called the Granite Building), was designed by architect John W. Roberts and constructed almost entirely of Colorado materials, primarily granite, rhyolite (lava stone) and red sandstone, sent

The Clayton Block, today called the Granite Building, replaced the original two-story brick building on the southern corner of Fifteenth and Larimer Streets. All four floors were leased by M.J. McNamara and Company; circa 1883. *History Colorado Collection.*

Before relocating to east Denver, Michael J. McNamara and his family occupied this two-story west Denver home at 1109 Eleventh Street (corner of Curtis Street) in the Auraria neighborhood. *Denver Public Library, Western History Collection.*

from quarries in Fort Collins, Coal Creek Canyon, Morrison and Manitou Springs. The first floor featured cast-iron pilasters, made by Colorado Iron Works, framing large sheets of plate glass. Inside, two elevators powered by steam connected all floors and were supplemented by a magnificent staircase made of ash, cherry and black walnut.[13]

The new home of M.J. McNamara & Company occupied the entire structure, from the basement to the fourth floor. Its staff numbered approximately 60, with more hired for the holiday season. (By 1886, the count had grown to 200, of whom 125 were dressmakers.) The first floor was filled with light, being fronted with glass on two sides. Colorful stained glass above each sheet of plate glass "produce[d] a very pretty effect in the room with its snowy white walls." One flight up, customers encountered the ladies' suit and shawl departments, along with an extensive collection of laces, embroideries, gloves, ribbons and other notions. An enormous Brussels carpet, in cream and cardinal red, created a feeling of luxury underfoot. The third floor housed the wholesale department; like other Denver department stores, McNamara shipped goods to stores in small towns throughout the state. The top floor housed the custom dressmaking department, and the basement featured "heavy goods," possibly carpets and furniture. The firm was highly regarded, and McNamara was known, perhaps due to his immigrant beginnings, as someone who would not turn away business from the humblest customer. Clerks were instructed to treat everyone with kindness, "from the poor woman who buys a spool of thread to the elegant lady who orders a $500 dress." With this retail palace, McNamara was now successful beyond his wildest dreams, and while no diaries or other sources survive that would indicate his state of mind, he was undoubtedly very proud of all he had accomplished in so short a time. Boom times will always instill feelings of euphoria and, inevitably, of invincibility.[14]

2

CALIFORNIA STREET

This man's fortune, could it have been meted out to him according to the manner of his deserving, should be counted by millions. As it stands, after many years of effort, he is rich only in the admiring esteem of all who know him, and in the memories of a well-spent life.[15]

THE FINEST DEPARTMENT STORE BUILDING WEST OF ST. LOUIS

When Michael J. McNamara opened his palatial store on the corner of Fifteenth and Larimer Streets in 1883, Larimer could still make a strong claim as Denver's "Main Street." City Hall, a grand stone structure replete with clock tower and bell, arose that same year a block to the southwest, at Fourteenth Street. Horace Tabor's magnificent office building, the Tabor Block (Denver's first five-story structure, featuring the city's first elevator), was only four years old, standing proudly one block northeast of McNamara's store, at Sixteenth Street, housing important businesses including the First National Bank. Farther up Larimer, the Windsor reigned as the city's finest hotel at Eighteenth Street. McNamara's location seemed ideal. But times were changing, and while Larimer Street would remain important to the city's businessmen for some time to come, Denver's ladies were finding its masculine environment less appealing. Also, Larimer was uncomfortably close to the city's notorious red-light district on Market Street, where upstanding women did not want to be seen. Stores catering to women, and finer stores generally, were therefore beginning to cluster on Lawrence Street, paralleling Larimer one block to the southeast. The corner of Lawrence and Sixteenth Streets was becoming a hub, home to Daniels and Fisher (earlier quartered on Larimer Street) since 1875, Leopold Guldman's Golden Eagle store since 1879 and menswear store Skinner Brothers and Wright since 1881. Not only was Lawrence Street less frenetic than Larimer, but thanks to the 1871 advent of a horsecar line (later electrified) that turned from Larimer onto Sixteenth Street, businesses were beginning to line Sixteenth, eager to take advantage of the pedestrian traffic generated by public transportation. Finally, the many corners on the shorter blocks of Sixteenth Street were better suited to the needs of large stores, which could garner more business with entrances on two sides instead of just one; a store with fronts on two streets made the most of its real estate and was more impressive. Larimer Street, with its longer blocks and narrow lots, would not be the center of town for much longer.

Early pioneer John J. Reithmann, a Swiss immigrant, had arrived in Denver City in 1858, the year of its founding, and set himself up as a druggist. By the 1880s, he was one of the city's best-known real estate barons and president of the German National Bank. He had built his home on the eastern corner of Sixteenth and California Streets, then a residential district. Diagonally across the street from his home, however, on land Reithmann also owned, a venue for roller-skating had sprung up in the mid-1880s, and with the new Arapahoe County Courthouse having recently been completed several blocks up Sixteenth, he knew his environs would become a business district before long. The Mammoth Rink, as it was known, was 125 feet deep by 150 feet wide along California Street. Under a ceiling illuminated by Chinese lanterns, genteel skaters glided to music provided by a live band; people of questionable character were banned. In addition to skating (admission was twenty-five cents, including skates), it offered thrilling demonstrations of bicycle and unicycle riders, along with occasional daredevil performers and orations by public figures.[16]

Reithmann knew McNamara from their business relationship—he was one of McNamara's several bankers. As recounted in later store-written histories, he approached McNamara with an outrageous idea: he should move his successful dry goods emporium from the busy corner of Fifteenth and Larimer Streets to Sixteenth and California, the site of the Mammoth Rink. Certainly, an ulterior motive would have been the enhancement of his own property values—not long after, he would sell his home site to Louis Mack, who erected a five-story office block on it in 1890. Also, it was clear by the second half of the 1880s that the city's well-heeled classes were moving farther southeast; a smart retailer would want to be as close to the best sources of trade as possible. He proposed to McNamara that he desert his still-new quarters on Larimer Street. He would build him, he said, "the finest department store building west of St. Louis, at Sixteenth and California."[17]

Was this folly? At the time, Daniels and Fisher, at Sixteenth and Lawrence Streets, was considered the city's finest department store, and the May Company at the same intersection (in the former Skinner Brothers and Wright building) was trying hard to become its busiest. Few merchants dared to venture farther southeast than Curtis Street, where John Jay Joslin's store had recently moved into a portion of the George Tritch Hardware building. While this California Street location was not, as later store histories recounted it, "out in the country," it was not exactly central—but Reithmann's instincts were right in sensing one day it would become the very heart of downtown. Undoubtedly, it was an unconventional choice for the moment, surrounded by residences and cottonwood trees.

The "finest department store building west of St. Louis," built in 1889 by John J. Reithmann for the McNamara Dry Goods Company, to a design by Frank E. Edbrooke, on the western corner of Sixteenth and California Streets. *Thomas J. Noel collection.*

View looking northeast along California Street showing the McNamara sign, just after The Denver Dry Goods Company had taken over management, circa 1894. *Denver Public Library, Western History Collection, photograph by Rose & Hopkins.*

In 1889, just six years after the Larimer Street palace had opened its doors, a three-story building of red pressed brick with limestone trim arose on the western corner of Sixteenth and California Streets. Its designer was Frank E. Edbrooke, at the time the city's most prolific commercial architect; he had arrived in 1879 to supervise the construction of the Tabor Block and then the Tabor Grand Opera House (both designed by his Chicago-based brother, Willoughby) and had since become the architect of choice for Denver's businessmen. His other extant works include the Brown Palace Hotel, the Oxford Hotel, the Masonic Temple Building and a few others; the majority of his creations have been demolished. While only three stories high (plus basement), the new structure was more than twice as wide along California Street as the old store's width on Larimer Street, giving it significantly more square footage. For its time, it was relatively utilitarian, with few architectural flourishes and built of materials humbler than those of the Clayton Block. At the curb, red sandstone hitching posts stood for the convenience of customers needing to tie up their horses.[18]

THE PANIC OF 1893

Filling such a large store with the same abundance of merchandise his Larimer Street emporium was known for cannot have been easy, but McNamara was up to the task, at first. His new store, with handsome mahogany and glass counters filling much of the first floor, was filled with the same kinds of wares he sold on Larimer for ladies, men, children and the home but on a far larger scale. An 1889 newspaper advertisement boasts that the store carried "the largest line of seal garments in the west" and was the "sole agent for the Judic Corset." It offered men's underwear at prices ranging from $1.25 to $3.50, in "fine natural wool," and ladies' Jouvin Gloves from $0.75 to $2.25.[19] Yet as time went on, the tone of his advertisements began to subtly change. In early 1892, McNamara advertised a $100,000 clearance sale, in which "Everything Goes," the entire stock being marked down. But that was mild compared to what would come eighteen months later.[20]

The Panic of 1893 was a worldwide economic depression. In Colorado, the primary impact came from the shift in silver demand after foreign governments ended their coinage of silver, much of which came from the state's mines; the repeal of the Sherman Silver Purchase Act in October of that year was the final nail in the coffin. The summer, particularly the month of July, saw the greatest effect in Denver, when a dozen banks failed, and millionaires like Horace Tabor lost their fortunes. Any financially overextended person or business was vulnerable, and that month's newspapers were filled with notices of bankruptcy and desperate pleas from many retail establishments begging their customers to shop, to help them raise enough cash to stay open. "The Greater Our Loss, The Greater Your Gain" framed the words *CASH SALE* in large letters in a McNamara advertisement on Sunday, July 16. "By making a big loss every day, so that every man, woman and child can see at a glance that we are sacrificing fully one-half the actual value throughout our entire stock, we have been able to keep our store filled during these trying, nervous times, with cash customers, and this is the class of people we particularly want to see to-morrow and throughout the coming week." Credit was fine for good times, but in bad times, cash ruled.[21]

McNamara's pleas were for naught: the company would not survive the troubled summer. Still burdened with more inventory than could be sold to nervous customers and faced with the demand by Union National Bank to immediately make good on a $75,000 loan, McNamara shut his doors, unable to pay Union or any of his other creditors, and the Arapahoe County sheriff auctioned off the store's contents on the morning of Thursday,

McNamara Dry Goods as seen from the Masonic Building (possibly from the roof), with store architect Frank E. Edbrooke's name visible in the distance on the side of the People's Bank Building at Sixteenth and Lawrence Streets, circa 1892. *Denver Public Library, Western History Collection, photograph by L.D. Regnier.*

September 7. There were a number of bidders, from Denver as well as New York. The winning bid of $132,500, submitted by representatives of Denver businessmen Dennis Sheedy and Charles B. Kountze, showed that the new owners had made a sharp bargain. Prior to the sale, the inventory had been valued at $298,000; adding fixtures, delivery wagons and horses to that made the firm worth a total of $310,000. Kountze was president of Colorado National Bank, and Sheedy was its vice-president. Colorado National (owed $97,500) was one of the largest of McNamara's creditors, so winning the bid allowed them to recoup the bank's losses and keep it from failing like so many others that year.[22]

In his autobiography, Sheedy makes no mention of the auction or of other bidders; the story he tells is somewhat different. After a hectic day and a night meeting of his banking colleagues, he recalls being asleep when his wife came to wake him because Kountze and McNamara were downstairs, along with the bank's attorneys: "I was told that the McNamara company was on the verge of collapse, and that we must be on hand early in the morning as attaching creditors to save our money." The men all drove in carriages to the store and engaged in an all-night negotiation. By morning, the plan was that Sheedy and Kountze would buy the store and pay off its other large banking creditor (City National Bank; he makes no mention of Union National). Its new name would be Sheedy & Kountze Dry Goods Company.[23]

The following Monday, September 11, the store reopened for a liquidation sale. Terms were "CASH and cash only," with the stated goal of garnering $200,000 in ninety days; the newspaper advertisement was signed "M.J. McNamara, Manager For Sheedy & Kountze." The doors opened promptly at 8:00 a.m., and the sales floor was immediately mobbed with "people of all classes and conditions of society," from "the poorest inhabitant of the [Platte River] bottoms to the most exacting leader of the most exclusive set on Capitol Hill" (whoever she might have been). McNamara presided over his store's demise, apparently relieved that his problems had come to a head and that he could now get on with living life; he "looked very happy as he greeted hundreds of friends who called to congratulate him," and he "spoke encouragingly of the future."[24]

Months passed and the holiday season came and went, with daily newspaper advertisements offering bargains to be had. They were still signed "M.J. McNamara, Manager for Sheedy & Kountze," with McNamara's name, so familiar to Denver shoppers, in a considerably larger type than the names of the new owners. As the spring of 1894 came, however, suddenly there was a change: McNamara's name was de-emphasized, with "Sheedy & Kountze" in a much larger font. It appeared that Sheedy & Kountze would be the permanent name for the new firm, but on May 22, 1894, newspapers announced an entirely new concern: The Denver Dry Goods Company, incorporated by Dennis Sheedy as president, Gustav C. Bartels as vice-president and Charles T. Austin as secretary and treasurer, to operate in the former McNamara building. Kountze was not mentioned as an officer, but he very likely still retained an ownership share (he was on the board of the new company), as did his Colorado National Bank.[25]

Sheedy's story will be told in the following chapter, but it is also important to remember Charles B. Kountze's role. He and his bank were well known in the city by the time he took over McNamara Dry Goods. Kountze was the youngest of four German brothers (in age order, they were Augustus, Herman, Luther and Charles), the sons of Christian Kountze of Saxony. They had opened Kountze Brothers Bank in fledgling Denver in 1862. Renamed Colorado National Bank in 1866, their bank would become an important Colorado institution, financing myriad developments in the state during its territorial years (which ended in 1876 with Colorado statehood) and for more than a century thereafter, until its purchase by a Minneapolis-

The Kountze Brothers Bank (later Colorado National Bank) on the western corner of Fifteenth and Market Streets, circa 1862. *Thomas J. Noel collection.*

based bank in 1998. Originally located on the western corner of Fifteenth and McGaa (later Market) Streets, Colorado National would eventually build a white marble "bank that looks like a bank" on the western corner of Seventeenth and Champa Streets, the heart of the "Wall Street of the West" (still standing, now repurposed as a hotel). For the first three decades of The Denver Dry Goods' existence, its fortunes would be closely intertwined with those of Colorado National Bank; its president, Charles B. Kountze; and his wife's relatives, the Berger family.[26]

Why did Sheedy choose the name "Denver Dry Goods," instead of Sheedy Dry Goods, or Sheedy & Kountze? Perhaps it was because the city had been so good to him that he wanted to honor it, or maybe he thought it would stand out among the competition, the only major Denver store not named for its owner, and with an eponymous name, instantly familiar to the citizens. Perhaps he was thinking "Sheedy" might sound too Irish at a time of widespread prejudice against that nationality. Perhaps Colorado National Bank, named for its state rather than its owners, served as a model. We will never know (his autobiography reveals only that "Denver had always appealed strongly" to him),[27] but with this name change, an institution was born.

Michael J. McNamara, after his namesake store had failed, stayed involved with Denver's mercantile trade because he was naturally good at it, even if the financial side was not his strong suit. Selling goods to customers, making friends along the way, had been his whole life. He went to work for his former rival, Daniels and Fisher, as a manager and then worked for another competitor, the May Shoe and Clothing Company (later simply May Company). He had long been involved with civic affairs, having helped to found the Denver Chamber of Commerce and Board of Trade, the 1880 National Mining and Industrial Exposition and what would become the Denver Public Library. In the years after his dry goods store failed, he would serve on the organizing committee of the annual Festival of Mountain and Plain, a grand autumn celebration meant to revive the spirits of the state's residents, traumatized by their sudden reversal of economic fortune in 1893, and he would continue to be a popular man about town. He died in 1904 in his home at 1353 Gaylord Street, surrounded by his wife, son and two daughters.[28]

3
ANOTHER IRISH MERCHANT

No business proposition is too great or too foreign to daunt him. If, in his judgment, the conditions are such that any man living can finance an enterprise and make it a success, his mental grasp of a situation and all the attending conditions are simply wonderful.[29]

THE CALL OF THE WEST

In some ways, Dennis Sheedy's early life was similar to that of Michael J. McNamara.[30] Born in Ireland on September 26, 1846, as the son of John Sheedy, a "gentle, refined and educated" farmer "in comfortable circumstances,"[31] and Margaret Fitzpatrick Sheedy, infant Dennis immigrated with his family to the United States after the Irish potato famine suddenly devastated their fortunes. Mrs. Sheedy had given birth to twelve children, although four had died by the time Dennis, the youngest, was born. Settling initially in Rockport, Massachusetts, in 1858 the family moved to Lyons, Iowa (now a section of Clinton, Iowa) on the Mississippi River, where his brother William had opened a store. William felt the family would have a better chance of prospering in wide-open Iowa, and convinced his parents to make the move. William, as well as Dennis's sister Johanna, both died about eight months after the family arrived, and heartbroken to have two more of his offspring pass away, John Sheedy died shortly thereafter. With the other siblings scattered, thirteen-year-old Dennis became the man of the family, pledging to take care of his mother and sister Ellen. He took a job working in a general merchandise store during the summer and attended school during the winter; he later credited his early retail experience as formative, giving him a "general knowledge of business"[32] that he would utilize throughout his life. At the outbreak of the Civil War, he tried to enlist as a Union soldier but was rejected due to his tender age.

In 1863, he, like McNamara a little later on, decided that the West held promise ("this was the call of the West, a call that must be answered," he later wrote, a recurring phrase in his autobiography) and came to

Irish immigrant Dennis Sheedy, who heeded "the Call of the West." *Denver Public Library, Western History Collection.*

Denver after a six-week overland journey from Omaha. Soon after arriving, he ran into Charles Pigott, an acquaintance from Lyons, and Pigott introduced him to a local merchant, Alvin B. Daniels, who operated a general store, Daniels and Brown, in partnership with J. Sidney Brown.[33] He worked for Daniels over the winter, sleeping in the store but taking his meals with Daniels and his wife, who treated him "as their son." He impressed Daniels with his energy and business acumen, but the restless Sheedy, still a teenager (though grown to six feet, two inches, and 160 pounds), dreamed of making huge profits in the risky business of overland freighting, a job that required not only business skills but, in those days, when hostilities with Native Americans prevented many wagon trains from safely reaching their destination, some degree of physical strength, bravery and willingness for confrontation. Daniels and his wife tried to persuade him to stay in Denver, but once they were convinced of his determination to embark on this new career, they "became most encouraging" and supported him wholeheartedly.[34]

Sheedy left the city in spring 1864 and embarked on a series of adventures that ultimately made him a rich man. Passing through Salt Lake City, he set out for Montana Territory, to the mining camp of Virginia City, where he "got the mining fever in its most virulent type" and was soon working for $6 per day wielding a pick and shovel.[35] With $800 saved from his work for Daniels, he bought a placer mine that eventually struck pay dirt and that he was able to sell for $2,200 soon after. That was the end of his mining career; he found it to be too financially risky. Taking his profits with him, he went to nearby Nevada, Montana, and opened a store with a partner named Gildersleeve. They ran it for just four months, making great profits, and then Sheedy was off again, to the Mormon settlement of Wellsville, Utah, where he operated another store. Within six months, he had sold $70,000 in merchandise, taking agricultural produce in exchange for goods. Needing to monetize the produce (much of it in the form of wheat, which he had ground into flour, sewing one thousand flour sacks himself), he realized he could make a killing by freighting the flour to Montana miners. After transporting the flour and other products to Virginia City, he had made a profit of $25,000, in frontier "currency" (gold dust).

Feeling he lacked proper education, Sheedy then spent the winter of 1865–66 in Chicago, enrolled in Eastman's Commercial College, where he learned business fundamentals. Upon graduating in the spring, he hatched a plan to sell Dutch ovens in the frontier West. He had noticed that open fireplaces were the universal way of cooking in Utah and Montana and so had 250 Dutch ovens, ideal for use with open fire, shipped from Albany, New York, to Fort Des Moines, Iowa, then the westernmost point of the nation's rail system. After leading a wagon train across the prairie (he had been elected captain due to his previous experience in the West), in Salt Lake City he sold the Dutch ovens, for which he had paid $30 apiece, for $125 to $175 each. Again he took flour instead of cash and decided to freight it, along with other goods, back to Virginia City, Montana. By the spring of 1867, he had sold his inventory and decided to open a general store in Lemhi City, Idaho, another placer mining camp then enjoying a boom.

The spring of 1868 found Sheedy in Helena, Montana, wholesaling groceries in partnership with two other men. (Their firm was called Corbin, Sherwood & Sheedy.) In the fall, he sold out and returned to Salt Lake City, intending to winter and then resume his profitable business of freighting goods to mining camps. But here, his life changed again (he was still only twenty-two years old) when he purchased three hundred head of cattle. He sold them to James Worthington, a cattleman who owned many more head, for which he needed a manager. He offered $2,000 per month to Sheedy to superintend the cattle and drive them to the lumber camps in the Sierra Nevada Mountains (where they served as food for the lumbermen who were providing the timber required for building the Central Pacific Railroad, the western end of the transcontinental railroad). This change began a lucrative career in which Sheedy engaged in the buying, driving and selling of cattle all over the western United States.

Cattle would form the basis of his fortune; over the course of the next dozen years, Sheedy bought and sold vast herds in Arizona, Texas, Kansas, Wyoming, Indian Territory (part of the future Oklahoma) and other western places. He held extensive ranchlands (fifty miles along the North Platte River) in Nebraska. In his autobiography, he devotes several pages to an 1878 episode in which he encountered difficulties in Kansas when the Northern Cheyenne, led by Chief Dull Knife, scattered his herds and killed some of his men. Sheedy organized a company of fifty or so armed white men to drive the Cheyenne away and regain control of his herd, but his force was too small. He was forced to ask Colonel Lewis of the U.S. Cavalry (stationed at Fort Dodge, Kansas) for help; Lewis engaged the Cheyenne in battle and was killed in action. Many years later, Sheedy obtained financial recompense from the Indian Depredation Claims Bureau for the loss of cattle during this episode. Finally, after a hard winter in 1879–80, in which he lost many head, he decided to get out of the cattle business entirely. Another factor was that the Great Plains, and the West generally, were being settled. Sheedy sensed the "complete passing of the great free, open range so necessary in the handling of such vast herds as I was handling."[36] He was no longer the strapping teenager, and he had made a lot of money. It was time to do something different.

Banking, Smelting and Owning a Department Store

In 1879, Alvin B. Daniels's wife died. Sheedy had remained good friends with the family, returning often to Denver to visit them during his cattle baron years. Mr. and Mrs. Daniels had had three children in the interim, one of them bearing the name George Sheedy Daniels (George and his sister, Olive, died as small children). Mrs. Daniels had extracted a promise from Sheedy that if she were to die he would "look after" her husband, and so the two men became even closer after her death. Then, in the fall of 1880, Daniels himself passed away, leaving the remaining son and heir, also named Alvin, bereft of both parents and still a minor. Sheedy came back to Denver to become his guardian.

Already wealthy, he still needed to be engaged in business—that was intrinsic to his nature. With cash from the sale of his cattle, Sheedy purchased stock in Colorado National Bank and became a director and its vice-president.[37] He forged a friendship and a business relationship that would endure until the ends of their lives with bank president Charles B. Kountze. Kountze appreciated Sheedy's distinctly conservative style of managing money and his determination that no debt should go unpaid. It was how Sheedy lived his own life, never owing money to anyone and, in turn, never allowing creditors to take advantage of his good nature. He acquired a reputation as a zealous protector of the bank's interests.

The bank, however, was not the primary source of his next fortune. That would come from his 1886 decision to buy a controlling interest in a failing ore processor, the Edward R. Holden Smelting Company, which had been in debt to Colorado National. In 1889, after injecting his money and personal energy into it, he reorganized his new concern as the Globe Smelting and Refining Company and grew it tenfold, until it was said to be the largest refiner of mineral ores in the United States, employing over one thousand men at its peak and processing 125 train carloads of ore daily. Knowing next to nothing of mineralogy when he took over Holden, Sheedy quickly learned all he could (helped by a tutor) and developed new, more efficient methods, eventually holding eighteen patents related to smelting. Around the vast Globe Smelter, which grew to occupy a huge plot of ground north of Denver, Sheedy developed a workers' community he called Globeville; the neighborhood's name is still in use today, although the smelter, which Sheedy sold to American Smelting and Refining Company in 1899, is gone. Sheedy was no Fezziwig when it came to managing his employees; according to historian Thomas J. Noel, he paid his men little. Common laborers made $1.75 for a ten-hour day, while skilled smelter workers earned only $2.50 to $3.50. One row of substandard homes in Globeville was informally christened "Sheedy Row," not necessarily an "honor."[38]

As for his ownership of The Denver Dry Goods, from the perspective of old age Sheedy knew it was the store, rather than his many other activities in life, for which he would be remembered. He wrote, "I have dwelt at considerable length upon this chapter of 'The Denver' as in these later years I have been more closely associated with the store, and perhaps more closely identified with it, than in any other enterprise, and I am proud of it."[39] Historian Phyllis J. Doner has concluded that Sheedy, similar to most of his Denver peers, "was not the urbane cosmopolitan retailer such as a John Wanamaker of Philadelphia" (Wanamaker was one of the most famous

Dennis Sheedy's Globe Smelting and Refining Company, located north of Denver near the South Platte River. *Author's collection.*

merchants in nineteenth-century America) but rather was "comfortable with and well suited to cope with the rough and tumble atmosphere of an early frontier community," an "[individualist] who sought adventure and challenge, dream[ing] of attaining wealth and…not hesitat[ing] to take risks to achieve that wealth." He "maintained firm control over The Denver Dry Goods Company for over twenty-nine years and ran the store as he would have bossed a wagon train, driven a herd of cattle or issued orders to workers at the Globe Smelter—with an iron grip."[40]

Sheedy led a busy personal life, too, once he settled down in Denver. In 1881, about the time he became Alvin Daniels's guardian, he married Catherine Vincentia Ryan, daughter of a Leavenworth, Kansas businessman. She bore him two daughters, Marie Josephine and Florence Elizabeth, but passed away in 1895. Three years later, Sheedy married a much younger woman, Mary Theresa Burke of Chicago, the niece of Bishop M.F. Burke of St. Joseph, Missouri. She gave birth to two sons who passed away in early childhood, but she would outlive him by more than three decades. His charitable contributions were many and included funds to help one of Denver's Irish Catholic parishes, St. Leo's in the Auraria neighborhood,

This page: Two postcard views of The Denver Dry Goods Company, the enterprise most closely associated with Dennis Sheedy. *Author's collection.*

Dennis Sheedy's magnificent residence at 1115 Grant Street in Denver's Capitol Hill neighborhood still stands, now repurposed as an office building. *History Colorado Collection.*

redeem itself out of foreclosure. In 1901, he was also listed as the largest donor to the Mount St. Vincent's orphanage in northwest Denver, and he gave repeatedly to St. Joseph's Hospital and the Cathedral (now Basilica) of the Immaculate Conception.[41]

Sheedy's extravagant and sprawling "Millionaire's Row" mansion, still standing at 1115 Grant Street in Capitol Hill, deserves special mention. He commissioned it during the heady boom year of 1890, hiring architect E.T. Carr of Kansas City, Missouri; it was completed in August 1892, less than a year before the panic. Three stories high, of red brick and red sandstone, the Queen Anne–style house features multiple chimneys, arches, gables, small balconies and dozens of windows in every size and shape; the detached building for stabling his horses was similarly grand. Inside, because Sheedy had "a love of nature,"[42] each room features a different species of wood, with paneling (by carpenter Joseph John Queree) matching the furniture. The first-floor rooms (music room, dining room, parlor and library) connected with sliding doors, so they could be thrown open for large gatherings. Big and bold, it was "an expression of the man's big, open life and of his originality."[43] Sheedy gave both of his daughters' hands in marriage in ceremonies held in the mansion. The 1911 wedding of his daughter Marie to New Yorker Robert L. Livingston was "one of the most fashionable ever held in Denver" according to the *New York Times*, and her sister's (Florence's) wedding to New Yorker I. Townsend Burden Jr. in 1915 would be celebrated by a telegram from the Pope. After Sheedy's death, his widow, Mary, lived in it for only a short time—she had no desire to live alone in such a large structure and moved to a smaller house nearby. By 1927, the Sheedy mansion had been repurposed as a music academy and boardinghouse, the Fine Arts School. In 1975, it was renovated into office space, its continuing use today.[44]

THE DENVER DRY GOODS COMPANY

An inquiry merely of curiosity…elicited from the manager the information that the class of goods on sale in this store is nothing less than a duplicate of the choice stock in the leading dry goods houses of New York and Chicago.[45]

GROWING WITH DENVER

Dennis Sheedy was a busy man, with his interests in Colorado National Bank, Globe Smelting and other enterprises, and he could not devote all of his time to managing his new department store, a more than full-time job. Therefore, at the bottom of the very first advertisement of The Denver Dry Goods Company on May 23, 1894, and for quite some time thereafter in all newspaper advertisements, there appeared the name "W.R. Owen, Manager." Sheedy explains that Owen was the "only one of the old McNamara staff that was retained in any kind of executive position," due to his and Charles B. Kountze's dissatisfaction with McNamara and his upper management and their esteem for Owen.[46]

William Roland Owen was a native of Fox Lake, Wisconsin, born to Welsh immigrants in 1852. At the tender age of thirteen, he began his retail career, working in country stores in Fox Lake, Racine and Portage, Wisconsin. In 1875, he came to Denver and worked for Daniels and Fisher as a traveling salesman for its wholesale operation but three years later decided to make his fortune in booming Leadville, Colorado, where he established his own dry goods store. In 1883, after selling out to

The Denver Dry Goods Company with its new fourth floor, festooned with bunting and the flags of many nations, circa 1905. *Thomas J. Noel collection.*

Daniels, Fisher and Smith (the Leadville branch of the Denver store), Owen came back to Denver and entered the wholesale fur business. In 1889, the year of the move to California Street, he bought an interest in M.J. McNamara Dry Goods, becoming its treasurer, and in that position, over the course of the following five years, became well acquainted with bankers Sheedy and Kountze. With the involuntary departure of Michael J. McNamara, he was the logical choice to head the new Denver Dry Goods Company—a natural merchant with a strong grounding in the fiscal side of the business.[47]

Owen wasted no time. Inheriting from McNamara Dry Goods a three-story (plus basement) building measuring 125 feet along Sixteenth Street and 175 along California Street, he began building up the business from the remains of the enterprise shattered by the Panic of 1893. By 1898, just four years after the firm's refounding, the building was already too small. Sheedy bought an additional two lots along California Street and commissioned Frank E. Edbrooke to design not only a 50-foot extension to match the original store (bringing its frontage along California Street to 225 feet) but also a fourth floor for the whole structure. The total cost was $50,000 (the

View down Sixteenth Street, with The Denver Dry Goods Company at left. Rivals A.T. Lewis and Son and May Company are visible in the distance to the left and right, circa 1906. *Library of Congress.*

equivalent of approximately $1.47 million today). At about the same time, The Denver Dry Goods Company also took over ownership of the original building and land from John J. Reithmann.[48]

The expanded store certainly impressed customers. The street-level floor was a warren of counters and departments, "a puzzling labyrinth of aisles that checquer the great floor like the streets of a city,"[49] with shoes for men and women, stationery and books, men's and women's furnishings, notions, confectionery, jewelry, linens, laces and gloves, silks and dress goods, each department "a veritable store in [itself]."[50] Above the main floor, ladies could enjoy a mezzanine reached by a broad stairway and furnished with comfortable seating, writing desks (with complimentary stationery) and toilet rooms, a place where they could rest or meet friends before heading to other floors to shop. On the second floor were departments for children; millinery ("hats without number, and of every description and style within the catalogue of fashion");[51] furs; cloaks and suits; the "art department,"

Views of the first floor, including the book department in 1902 (*above*) and the notions department in 1898 (*below*). *Jim O'Hagan collection.*

Views of the second floor, including the millinery department (*above*) and the art department (*below*), 1898. *Jim O'Hagan collection.*

featuring various decorative items for the proper Victorian home; and private offices for store management. On three, shoppers would find carpets, draperies and furniture, along with workrooms to customize these items to suit customers' tastes and needs. The new fourth floor was primarily given over to dress workrooms, necessary in an era when ladies' wardrobes were far more complex than they are today; much tailoring was necessary for customers to be properly fitted, and it was common to have the entire dress sewn on-site from dry goods purchased at the store. Not to be forgotten, the basement featured china, glass and silver, toys, coffee and tea. Two passenger elevators connected all floors.

Four years after the expansion, in early 1902 Sheedy paid $71,000 for an additional three lots along California Street, a hefty sum for its time that showed that Denver's economy had recovered from the Panic of 1893. Sheedy intended to expand all the way to Fifteenth Street, which would make The Denver the largest department store in the city, surpassing Daniels and Fisher. But he was prevented from doing so until he could buy the remaining four lots that separated his property from Fifteenth. Real estate prices were heating up so quickly that by the fall of 1902, he would find himself spending $150,000 for just the two lots at the Fifteenth Street end of the block. The two lots in between this corner and the three he had bought earlier in the year took some longer amount of time to procure, so he was prevented from adding onto the store until 1906. By this time, thanks to streetcar lines built on Fifteenth in the late 1880s and 1890s, most chamber of commerce members (of whom Sheedy was one) felt that the street would become as important to Denver's business life as the retail-dominated Sixteenth and the finance-dominated Seventeenth. Sheedy, with his bank on Seventeenth and his store on Sixteenth, did not want to miss out.[52]

The new 1906 addition, built at a cost of $315,000 (about $6.42 million today) and occupied and opened in 1907, was of a different style from the original building and its 1898 addition, although Frank E. Edbrooke once again designed it. Instead of Victorian commercial, with tall, narrow windows connected by limestone bands, the new wing, six stories tall, would feature impressively large windows on all floors, bringing more light into the interior and looking far less fussy from the street. Like the older building, it would be of red pressed brick, with plate glass show windows on the ground floor to entice passersby. Altogether, the store could now boast 650 linear feet of show windows, lined with 1,200 feet of solid mahogany paneling and leaded-glass clerestory windows that allowed outdoor light to reach interior departments. The new wing enabled all sales floors to be

CORSET DEPARTMENT—Continued.

P. D. Corsets.

P. D. Corsets, white and drab sateen, "a leader," regular $3.00 quality, $1.49.

157 — P. D. — Short Length, white, drab and black, at $3.00.

248—P. D.—Medium Length, white, drab and black, at $3.00.

97 — P. D. — Extra Long, white, drab and black, at $3.75.

904—P. D.—Medium Waist, long over hips and abdomen for stout figures, black only, at $6.00.

Jean d'Arc, for stout figures, medium waist, extra long over hips and abdomen, with webbing abdominal band, drab, $5.50; black, $7.00.

35—J. B. Corset, summer net, medium, French model, at $1.75.

36—J. B. Corset, sateen, medium, French model, white, $1.75; black, $2.00.

12—J. B. Corsets, medium length, pink and blue, at $1.00.

W. B. Corsets.

W. B.—451—Medium waist, long hip, drab and black sateen, at $1.25.

W. B.—402—Medium waist, long hip, drab and black sateen, at $1.75.

W. B.—155—Cyclist, medium waist, short elastic hip, white, drab and black, $1.50.

W. B.—656—Medium length, white, drab and black sateen, at $2.00.

W. B. — 254 — Heavily boned, long waist, short hip, white and black, at $2.75.

W.B.—126— Long Waist, white, drab, and black sateen, at $3.00.

W. B.—303—Six-hook, extra length, white and black, at $3.00.

W. B. — 626 — White Satin Ribbon Corset, medium length, suitable for bridal trousseaus, at $12.00.

When ordering Corsets please specify waist measure over dress.

A page from an 1898 mail order catalogue shows a variety of available corsets for the well-fitted woman. *Jim O'Hagan collection.*

A view of the basement level in 1902. *Jim O'Hagan collection.*

The Frank E. Edbrooke–designed 1906 addition nearing completion. *Denver Public Library, Western History Collection; photograph by Harry Mellon Rhoads.*

expanded and for executive offices to be centralized on the new sixth floor. For the first time, The Denver would offer meals, with a tearoom opening on the fourth floor of the new building in 1907 (The Denver's Tea Room's full history is told in chapter 6). The Denver was now the only store in the city that could boast frontage on two major business streets, Sixteenth and Fifteenth, along with a 400-foot first-floor main aisle, an impressive length that it would claim (with questionable veracity, but with typical Denver boastfulness) was the longest department store aisle in the United States. Total square footage now came to 322,830.[53]

This made The Denver Dry Goods, all of twelve years old, the largest store in Denver, in Colorado and in several surrounding states. To put this signal accomplishment in context, Daniels and Fisher had grown many times its original size since it relocated to Sixteenth and Lawrence Streets in 1875 but could not grow further along Lawrence Street without buying and demolishing another half block of buildings (including the busy Markham Hotel). It was only about half as large as The Denver in 1906. Even after

On the roof of the addition, note the horse and knight, which were outlined in light bulbs at night during the 1913 Thirty-Second Triennial Conclave of the Knights Templar, as viewed from Welton and Fifteenth Streets. *Denver Public Library, Western History Collection; photograph by George L. Beam.*

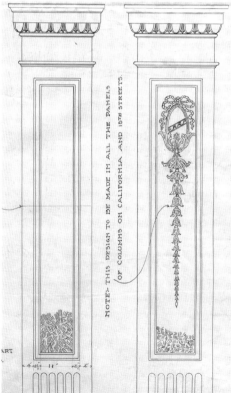

Above: "Bess," the delivery horse poses with William Hoffman. In this image, you can see the decorative entrance canopy featured on the 1906 addition. *Denver Public Library, Western History Collection.*

Left: An original drawing from the office of architect Frank E. Edbrooke shows the cartouches on the first floor columns. *Jim O'Hagan collection.*

THE DENVER DRY GOODS

D. SHEEDY, President
W. R. OWEN, Vice-Prest. and Manager
H. J. BAGLEY, Secretary and Treasurer

COMPANY

DENVER
COLORADO

A Progressive Modern Department Store and Mail Order House

"THE DENVER" NOW HOLDS CLEAR TITLE TO ITS POSITION AS THE LARGEST STORE IN THE WEST.

The floor area is over 300,000 square feet, exclusive of the five story and basement brick warehouse at Twelfth and Wazee Streets.

The Main Aisle is 20 feet wide, extending directly through from Sixteenth to Fifteenth Streets.

The entire store, both the old part and the new, is finished throughout with solid mahogany fixtures of the latest type.

THE IMMENSE STOCK OF MERCHANDISE HAS BEEN SELECTED—AND ALWAYS WILL BE SELECTED—TO MEET THE REQUIREMENTS OF ALL THE PEOPLE OF WHATEVER SOCIAL STATION. Those of ample means will find the world's choicest manufactured products assembled here in fascinating variety, while patrons with more modest resources can depend upon almost endless assortments of good goods, honestly priced, and every article sold with The Denver's unqualified guarantee of proper quality, or money refunded upon request.

A 1907 mail order catalogue bragged of The Denver's status as "the largest store in the west." *Jim O'Hagan collection.*

By the early 1920s, The Denver's (left) rivals included, on the left side of Sixteenth Street, the Neusteter Company across the alley from the store, A.T. Lewis and Son and Joslin's. On the right side, the store competed with Gano-Downs, May Company and Daniels and Fisher, with its iconic tower. *Author's collection.*

it expanded across the alley in 1910–11 and built its famous tower on the corner of Sixteenth and Arapahoe Streets, Daniels and Fisher's total square footage would not equal The Denver's. May Company, which that same year (1906) had moved to sparkling new quarters at Sixteenth and Champa Streets, was much smaller and, even with additions in 1925 and 1940, would never equal The Denver in size. Joslin's occupied a five-story building that filled only four lots at Sixteenth and Curtis Streets; John Jay Joslin had been selling dry goods in Denver since 1873, four years before Edgar Drew and Michael J. McNamara formed their partnership, but Joslin's would remain small. Present and future rivals Golden Eagle, A.T. Lewis and Son, Gano-Downs, Neusteter Company and the short-lived Steel's would never come close to The Denver in size. It was only in 1958, when May-D&F, formed by the buyout of Daniels and Fisher by May, moved into its new Courthouse Square quarters at Sixteenth and Tremont Streets, that The Denver would see a rival come close to equaling it in square footage. For decades, The Denver Dry Goods Company was the unquestioned reigning retail monarch of the Queen City of the West.[54]

CATERING TO THE CUSTOMER

The Denver was not only expanding physically—under Owen's direction, and in competition with other merchants, it was also finding new ways to please its customers and instill loyalty. In 1899, it built a "fine new barn" at Twelfth and Curtis Streets for its growing fleet of horse-driven delivery wagons. Other stores had similar services, but horses would shortly give way to automotive transport. In 1901, The Denver would establish itself as the first city store with motorized delivery when it purchased two steam engine–powered White Automotive Company trucks (the initial one the store bought was White's first-ever production truck). Soon they were noisily chugging their way through the streets, probably to the delight of children and grown men, causing dogs to bark and neighbors to look out their windows to see who was getting a delivery. With curved bonnet tops sheltering the driver, wire-spoke wheels and the store's name prominently painted on the sides, they also served as a highly visible form of advertising. In 1910, after gasoline engines emerged as the dominant automotive technology, The Denver bought a fleet of twenty-six Model T–based trucks from a local Ford agency, O'Meara Company. This brought further name recognition for the store, as someone, either from its publicity department or (more likely) that of Ford Motor Company, sent photographs of the fleet to newspapers around the world, many of which published them.[55]

Another early innovation, which would last for many decades, was the Lost-and-Found Book, a large loose-leaf journal bound in red leather, located on a stand inside the Sixteenth Street entrance. The store's name was printed at the top of each page, along with the words "Notify your friends in what department they may find you," and it became a very popular medium for that purpose. People tended to use initials, first names or nicknames rather than last names, and store staff kept a close eye on the pages to ensure that mischief-makers scrawled nothing naughty. Typical messages might read, "Dot and I have gone to get a pair of jeans," or "Mamie: I'm downstairs in men's underwear. Bess." The family member who had parked the car might leave a message indicating where it was parked or when the meter would expire. Sometimes people would leave multiple messages for one another over the course of an hour or two, like ships passing in the night. Once, the store received a telegram explaining that a certain person would be waiting by the book and to please tell that person that her party, traveling from another state,

The store's original horse-drawn delivery wagon (*above*), seen here near the western bank of Cherry Creek, was replaced in 1901 by two steam-powered White Automotive Company trucks (*below*), photographed at the Colorado Capitol Building. *Above, Jim O'Hagan collection; below, Linda Lebsack collection.*

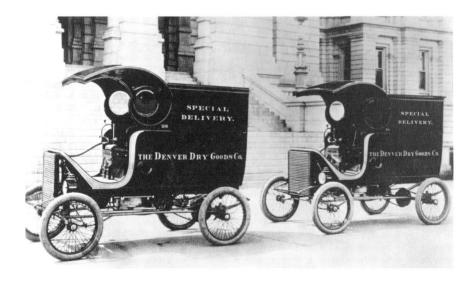

In 1907, the store unveiled its first escalator, an up-only machine that conveyed shoppers to the second floor. *Denver Public Library, Western History Collection, photograph by Louis Charles McClure.*

had been detained. A staff member managed to find the person and give her the message.[56]

When the new Fifteenth Street wing opened in June 1907, management made some changes to the older parts of the building. One of the biggest improvements was the store's first escalator, which carried shoppers up from the first to the second floor. There was only one; to come back down or to visit other floors, stairs or elevators were still necessary. On its first day of operation, and for several days afterward, a small orchestra played music to soothe the nerves of first-time riders. In later publicity materials, the store claimed it was the first escalator in the city, not admitting (or perhaps misremembering) that it was actually the second—the first had been installed in the new May Company store on Champa Street that opened in late 1906, beating The Denver by six months.[57]

WORKING AT THE DENVER

Although Dennis Sheedy and manager William R. Owen had established a traditional hierarchical staff structure when they began operating the store as The Denver Dry Goods Company in 1894, with department heads reporting to Owen and each department structured as a miniature version of the larger store (essentially like any department store of its day), once in a while Sheedy and Owen carried their ideals a bit far. In 1902, they established a new rule for female employees (adult female salespeople and girls employed to run customers' cash from departments to the central cashier) that was designed to "do away with the clash of colors behind the counters and the cheap overdressing of the ill-advised younger girls." Sheedy and Owen were concerned that the staff, by wearing flashy clothing, were "[clashing] horribly with the high-class goods they have to handle" and were at risk of alienating shoppers by wearing cheap, gaudy imitations of what their customers wore—clothing that "might be in place at 'social dances'" but not in the store's refined quarters. The new rule specified that all female staff would, from September 15 forward, wear only two colors: all black in winter and all white in summer.[58]

The store claimed that "all the high-class stores of the East have adopted this plan," but some female staff were not having it. In many cases it meant purchasing almost an entirely new wardrobe, and some saw a double standard in male counterparts not being forced to adopt a similarly staid dress code. Describing the men, one anonymous woman said:

> They come down in big check suits that "clash" as hard with the goods they handle as anything I know of, and behind the same counter will be a man in a badly washed linen outfit, stretched all out of shape, and another in frock coat, white vest, gray trousers and a blue tie. And out in the aisle the floorwalker will be walking around with a light tweed plaited hunting jacket and trousers turned up around the bottoms an inch, although it will have been a week since the floors were wet by the scrubbers.[59]

This woman would not complain about having to wear only black attire, she told a reporter, if the men were made to do the same. The rule remained in place for many years, as evidenced by a circa 1941 employee manual: "Saleswomen should wear a plain, business-like dress in navy blue or black, *solid color*. A white blouse with sleeves may be worn with either navy or black

The umbrella department on the first floor, probably before the 1902 dress code dictated solid black or white for female staff. *Denver Public Library, Western History Collection.*

skirts. During the summer months, an all white dress may be worn." (The manual still listed no requirements for men.)[60]

Despite rules of this nature, from its earliest days The Denver tended to retain its staff for a very long time and, for store anniversaries, would publicize its longer-serving employees. A 1923 article listed a number of staffers who had been around since the days of Michael J. McNamara. Miss Kathryn M. Bennett, buyer for toiletries, drugs, jewelry and hairdressing, had served since 1888 but was bested by her colleague Thomas H. Protheroe, buyer for linens and domestics, who had begun working for Drew and McNamara in the original two-story red brick Clayton Block, in 1879 (forty-four years). Other longtimers highlighted in the piece include L. Blanchard (1881), William Hoffman (1886), Laura Larson (1888), Joe Sullivan (1890, changed from opening carriage doors for customers originally to automobile doors), Joseph MacDonald (head cashier, 1890), Hugh Shields (book and stationery buyer, 1892), William Grams (window dresser, 1892) and John Murray (1893). This tradition of celebrating employees' longevity would continue.[61]

How well were people compensated in those days? A December 1923 monthly operations report shows a total payroll of 1,491 persons (inflated

Two views of the first floor in 1898, showing the cut glass and stationery departments (*above*) and the glove, handkerchief and lace department (*below*). *Jim O'Hagan collection.*

Two views of the second floor, showing a panorama of various departments in 1902 (*above*) and the cloak and suit department in 1898 (*below*). *Jim O'Hagan collection.*

A Section Across Drapery and Carpet Departments, Third Floor

West Section
Drapery Department
Third Floor

East Section Carpet Department, Third Floor

Carpet Department from Corner California and 15th Streets, Third Floor

A Glimpse of Our Carpet and Drapery Departments

These departments join on the third floor and together occupy a floor space
125x175 feet, an area far in excess of that given to these lines by any other
Colorado store. The third floor section of our Furniture Department occupies
all other space on this floor, making a total length of 400 feet.

VISIT US WHEN IN THE CITY

This 1915 mail-order catalogue page shows the third-floor carpet and drapery departments
from various angles. *Jim O'Hagan collection.*

by 200 to 300 for the holiday season), earning an average weekly wage of $18.74, or about $577 in today's values, pretax. This figure masks significant differences among the various types of workers, the vast majority (1,270) of whom were classified as clerks; roughly half of these were "selling clerks," earning $17.52 weekly ($540 today), and the remainder were "non selling clerks," earning $15.09 weekly ($465 today). The 31 employees classified as buyers, on the other hand, were quite well compensated, earning an average of $92.48 weekly ($2,850 today). Managers and their assistants, numbering 22, only made about half as much as the all-important buyers, earning $45.72 weekly ($1,410 today). The 168 skilled workers in the store's manufacturing departments (dressmaking, alterations and saddle-making) were better paid than the clerks, earning an average of $20.05 weekly ($618 today). Like most retail establishments, the store never paid its employees more than it had to; after World War II, workers feeling the pinch of postwar inflation would let management know exactly how they felt about its compensation.[62]

IN FULL FLOWER

*We come to Denver because we believe in this city
and believe in the possibilities of this establishment.*[63]

NEW OWNERSHIP

William R. Owen died in 1918 at the age of sixty-six and was replaced as manager by Hugh L. MacWhirter, a veteran employee. A more momentous death occurred on October 16, 1923, when seventy-seven-year old Dennis Sheedy passed away. He had been suffering from pneumonia but had kept working, both at The Denver and Colorado National Bank, until ten days before his death. He left an estate estimated to be worth $2 million, or the equivalent of about $416 million at today's valuation. His will split the fortune equally, with one third going to his widow, Mary, and one third each to his daughters, Marie and Florence, and set up trusts for his seven grandchildren (Mary would outlive him for three-plus decades, passing away on December 25, 1958).[64]

With the owner deceased, and his heirs not interested in active management of a busy department store, someone with vision was required to pilot the ship going forward. Colorado National Bank still held a significant block of stock, so its president at the time, George O. Berger, took over briefly as leader until a more permanent solution could present itself. Mary Sheedy knew that her late husband had been friendly with Melvin L. Wilkinson, president of a St. Louis department store called Scruggs, Vandervoort and

A 1940s view of the Denver Dry Goods Company from the roof of the Mack Block diagonally across the intersection of Sixteenth and California Streets. Note the white paint obscuring the original brick and limestone. *Thomas J. Noel collection.*

Barney, and she asked him if his firm would be interested in purchasing The Denver. Negotiations proceeded apace, and on February 14, 1924, just four months after Sheedy's death, the St. Louis store announced it would buy The Denver Dry Goods Company for $5 million. This amount covered the stock held by the Sheedy heirs, as well as additional stock owned by Colorado National and Berger. In addition to the St. Louis store, Scruggs, Vandervoort and Barney (usually just called "Vandervoort's" by St. Louis shoppers) also owned a St. Louis bank, a St. Louis jewelry store and G.L. White Dry Goods of Columbus, Ohio.[65]

This was the 1920s, a period when local stores across the country were combining into chains across multiple cities, their mergers fueled by the easy credit available in that boom decade. Denver's own May Company, after its 1877 Leadville birth and subsequent move to Denver, had as early as 1892 become a chain of two after it bought the Famous Company in St. Louis (later merging it with William H. Barr to create Famous-Barr and moving May headquarters to that city) and by the 1920s had additional stores in Cleveland, Akron and Los Angeles. In 1910, John Jay Joslin had sold his Denver store to the forerunner of Mercantile Stores Company, a chain with operations across the Midwest. In 1922, a short-lived national chain department store arrived in Denver, Steel's, building a four-story Grecian-inspired edifice one block from The Denver at Sixteenth and Welton Streets. By this time, F.W. Woolworth, the national chain of five-and-ten-cent stores, already had multiple Denver locations, as did James Cash Penney's chain of moderately priced department stores. Sears, Roebuck and Montgomery Ward had also established Denver stores (Ward's included a massive multistory distribution warehouse on South Broadway for its mail-order business). These were just the local manifestations of national trends; the 1920s were a time for national chains to grow, so it was not surprising that the city's largest store would change hands so easily after the founder's death.[66]

Wilkinson appointed his chief lieutenant (and son-in-law), Frank M. Mayfield, as general manager of The Denver, and the new men took advantage of the general prosperity to usher the store into a golden era,

In 1924, new owners Scruggs, Vandervoort and Barney added two more floors to the building. *Denver Public Library, Western History collection.*

building on what Sheedy had created to develop the great store that generations of Denverites would know and love. Assuring shoppers that there would be no change of name, policy or personnel in the firm, the new men promised changes (not yet specified) that would allow them to double the trade within five years. Although the ownership transfer did not take place until late March 1924, by that year's holiday shopping season, the new owners had already made a huge improvement: the addition of two more floors to the Sixteenth Street building. The new fifth floor (the "upper fifth") housed a relocated tearoom, moving up from the fourth floor of the Fifteenth Street building, while the new sixth became the new executive office floor. The two new levels allowed for not only a larger foodservice business (described in the next chapter) but also the addition of new departments and enlargements of old ones throughout the building.[67]

A Vast Array

What was it like shopping at The Denver Dry Goods Company by this time? It had undergone three significant expansions since Michael J. McNamara had opened his three-story emporium in 1889, and the store then owned by Scruggs, Vandervoort and Barney could boast a vast array of goods and services to satisfy the needs of its middle- and upper-class clientele.

The first floor, bisected by the famous four-hundred-foot-long main aisle, featured an array of counters for women's cosmetics, toiletries, handbags, gloves, handkerchiefs, scarves, umbrellas, hosiery, jewelry, casual millinery and knit underwear. Additional departments for women included budget hosiery, blouses and "pin money" dresses. The female home economist could stock up on piece goods in cotton or silk, along with notions, laces, buttons, ribbons and patterns to sew her own clothing. The first floor was also home to all of the departments catering to The Denver's male customers, including men's clothing, suits, neckwear, shirts, socks, underwear and shoes. This high-traffic street floor also included books and magazines, stationery, cameras and "Hoover Sweepers" (vacuum cleaners), along with counters for drugs, baked goods and candy. There was additionally a central wrap desk for customers' purchases, a ticket booth for theatergoers and a watch and clock repair counter. The mezzanine balconies overlooking the first floor continued to feature areas for female shoppers to rest and socialize, along

Above: The first floor is packed with shoppers; note the two new elevators (center) and the store's handsome clock (top right). *Linda Lebsack collection.*

Right: A 1927 fashion show invitation. *Author's collection.*

An Invitation

from the Denver Dry Goods Co. *to a*

Private Showing and Selling

of Misses' Street and Afternoon

FROCKS

at **$37.**⁰⁰

TUESDAY, FEBRUARY FIFTEENTH

Foremost Paris and New York fashions for those who seek the beautiful, the unusual, the marked individuality.

Composé, Bow Frocks and other important Spring 1927 style innovations, utterly smart to the last exquisite detail.

Tuesday,
February 15th
1927

The Denver Dry Goods Co.

Shown Only in The French Room
Second Floor

with offices for various departmental buyers, the store's personal shopper and a portrait photography studio.[68]

Boarding the store's lone escalator, shoppers ascended to a second floor entirely devoted to the needs of women. There was a Casual Shop, a Gown Shop and a Home and Town Shop, along with departments for dresses in popular prices, more expensive dresses and sportswear. There were shoes, millinery, corsets, lingerie, coats, suits and a fur salon (along with a fur repair shop). The second floor also boasted a bridal shop, and a department for "special sizes" (referred to as "Stout Wear" in an internal document but not, presumably, by floor personnel). Buyers for these departments had offices tucked into various corners, as did the store's fashion coordinator.

On the third floor, shoppers could find complete departments for furnishing every room in the house, from the parlor to the bedroom, along with clothing departments for children of every age: infants' wear, boys' wear, girls' wear, the Junior Shop and the High School Shop, along with

A shopper browses the WPA's American Guide Series display in the book department, circa 1937. *Denver Public Library, Western History Collection, photograph by the Works Progress Administration.*

The L-shaped display window at Sixteenth and California Streets, probably during the 1930s. *History Colorado Collection.*

appropriate shoes to wear at those ages. The third floor was also where shoppers with house accounts could pay their bill.

The fourth floor was the last one where the Sixteenth Street and Fifteenth Street sides met contiguously on the same level. Here were myriad departments for completing the home: draperies, rugs, floor coverings ("linoleums"), linens and domestics, hardware, paints and small and major electric appliances. Once they became household necessities, there were radios, too. This floor also housed an interior decorating department to help the homeowner coordinate the various purchases necessary for furnishing a house; the city was undergoing one of its periodic residential building booms during the 1920s, with vast new tracts opening in diverse locations such as Park Hill, University Park, Bonnie Brae and other desirable neighborhoods, and The Denver Dry Goods sold everything these new homes needed. Just above the fourth floor of the Sixteenth Street building, a mezzanine floor contained back-of-house operations including stock storage for china, glass, silver and other departments.

The Denver's furniture department is highlighted in this 1920s window display; note the leaded glass above, which allowed daylight to penetrate the store's interior, and glass blocks embedded in the sidewalk, allowing light to reach vaults below. *Denver Public Library, Western History Collection, photograph by Harry Mellon Roads.*

Ascending to the fifth floor of the Fifteenth Street building, a customer could add grace notes to daily living, for here were the departments for art needlework, china, glass, tabletop, lamps and gifts, along with luggage and the new beauty salon. Upstairs, executive offices occupied the new sixth floor of the Sixteenth Street building, while the Fifteenth Street side housed the candy kitchen and Stockmen's Store (both of which are described in a later chapter), along with operational departments, such as advertising, display, carpentry, painting, shipping, will call, mail order and an infirmary staffed by a nurse. Downstairs, below street level, the Budget Store contained many of the same departments found upstairs, along with a post office substation (with a counter for stamp and coin collectors) and a shoe repair shop. Away from the downtown facility, the store operated a large six-story warehouse on Wazee and Twelfth Streets in Auraria (it still stands, now with an Auraria Parkway address), along with off-site carpet and drapery workrooms, a radio repair shop, an upholstery shop and a garage (at Twelfth and Curtis Streets, the original stables) housing its fleet of delivery vehicles.

The Denver Dry Goods Company warehouse still stands at Twelfth and Wazee Streets (the latter now Auraria Parkway), circa 1933. *Denver Public Library, Western History Collection.*

Truly, The Denver epitomized the old department store model of "something for everyone," very dissimilar to the pared-down suburban department stores remaining in the twenty-first century. To keep shoppers well fueled for a full day of shopping, The Denver opened the largest restaurant in the city on the new upper fifth floor, a tearoom that created wonderful memories for generations of Colorado residents.

6

THE TEA ROOM

To those hundreds who thronged the new Fifth Floor Tea Room yesterday—we thank you! Although we had been planning very carefully for this opening day—although we were thoroughly prepared to handle capacity crowds—Still—we were NOT prepared for the overwhelming response accorded to this fine, new service to the people of Denver.[69]

THE HEART OF THE DENVER

When people today recount their memories of The Denver Dry Goods, the store's massive fifth-floor restaurant, the Tea Room, invariably becomes the focus of conversation. If the store was the "heart of Denver," as discussed in the introduction, then the Tea Room was "the heart of the heart" of Denver. It was not the cuisine so much that made it memorable. The food was good, certainly, but would not win awards for culinary innovation: dishes were familiar, sold at reasonable prices, with no challenging flavors or exotic ingredients. The store didn't use the phrase, but today its offerings would be affectionately termed "comfort food."

Rather, the Tea Room is remembered as a tradition and as a Denver institution. It was the largest restaurant in the city and was *the* place where friends met for lunch, where businessmen crafted deals, where fashion shows entertained and enticed, where busy shoppers took sustenance before tackling another floor and where countless children were entertained by dolls' tea parties and breakfasts with Santa. For most of The Denver's history, going to the Tea Room was a special occasion, calling for men to wear good suits and women to don fine hats and white gloves. When the store closed in 1987, people would find other places to buy clothing, housewares and furniture, but there would be no replacement for the Tea Room.

The tearoom that people remember was not the store's first, nor was The Denver Dry Goods home to the earliest department store tearoom in the city (Daniels and Fisher had opened one previously). The Denver's first full-service tearoom opened in 1907, on the fourth floor of the Fifteenth Street building. Prior to that year, a small area on the second floor had served tea and refreshments, but was not a full restaurant.[70] It, too, was a large facility, seating five hundred for breakfast, lunch or dinner, an "attractive, restful and completely satisfactory place" where "popular prices prevail[ed]."[71] The tearoom that came to be such an important Denver institution opened as part of Scruggs, Vandervoort and Barney's 1924 two-floor addition to the store on the Sixteenth Street side of the building. This fifth-floor facility was located on the "upper" fifth floor, so called because unlike the basement

The fifth-floor Tea Room, at the time of its 1924 opening. *Denver Public Library, Western History Collection.*

Two women take a break from shopping, circa 1940s. *Linda Lebsack collection.*

and first four floors, which were all at the same elevation in both buildings, it was set higher than the fifth floor in the Fifteenth Street building; a stairway connected it to the lower fifth floor in that wing.

The new Tea Room opened on Friday, November 28, 1924. Seating eight hundred, opening-day crowds proved to be more than the facility could handle—although approximately 3,500 meals were served that day, management had to turn hundreds more away during the lunch crush. The room, while very large, was gracious and elegant, with a vaulted ceiling supported by a forest of octagonal columns. Along the California Street and Sixteenth Street sides, French doors opened onto a deep balcony, the Promenade, where patrons could stroll before or after their meal. The room initially featured an ivory and blue color scheme, with blue draperies and upholstery. Furniture was crafted of oak. To speed diners to the upper fifth floor, the store installed two more elevators, operated as expresses, not stopping on lower floors.[72]

For men, the Tea Room featured the separate glass-enclosed Grill Room on the Sixteenth Street end, strictly a stag environment, with no women allowed other than waitstaff, at least in the early days. The Grill Room sat approximately 150, with two large round tables prominent. One table was reserved for store executives, while the other was home to the city's old

Opposite: The Tea Room's menu from the late 1940s. *Jim O'Hagan collection.*

Below: This double postcard shows the Tea Room, the outdoor promenade and the waiting area, circa 1924. *Thomas J. Noel collection.*

VIEWS OF THE DENVER DRY GOODS COMPA

A Section of the Spacious Tea Room..

Californi Pr Rock) Mou.

SOUPS and APPETIZERS

Chicken Broth with Rice
Cup....15   Bowl....25

Cup of Consomme....15	Soup du Jour....15
Chilled Juices: Tomato, Grapefruit or Pineapple....15	
Frosted Fruit Juice....15	Chilled Melon (In Season)
Frosted Fruit Cup....20	Cantaloupe 15
	Honeydew Melon 20
Half Grapefruit 15	Watermelon 20

SANDWICHES

Egg Salad 35	Fig and Nut on Toast....25
Virginia Baked Ham,	Tearoom Special Club House
Saratoga Chips 55	Two Layer....75
Cold Roast Prime	Three Layer....95
Rib of Beef 75	Peanut Butter....25
Lettuce, Tomato and	Swiss Cheese 50
Bacon on Toast....55	Chicken Salad 55
American Cream Cheese	Sliced Chicken....70
on Toast 30	Smoked Beef Tongue 50

SALADS

Raw Vegetable Salad with Cottage Cheese....50	
Lettuce and Tomato, French Dressing....50	
Stuffed Tomato with Chicken....80	
Special Whole Fruit Plate, Bread and Butter Sandwich....80	
Tearoom Chicken Salad with Tomato Slices....80	
Our Special Tearoom Salad Plate....1.00	

DESSERTS

Home-made Cake ....15; a la Mode 25	
Home-made Pie ....20; a la Mode 30	
Our Own Made Ice Cream, Vanilla, Strawberry or Chocolate....15	
Oriental, Chocolate or Butterscotch Sundae....25	
With Nuts 30	
Cherry, Lime or Orange Flavored Pineapple Sherbet....15	
Strawberry, Raspberry or Banana Shortcake,	
A la Mode or Whipped Cream....25	
Banana Split 45	
Pineapple, Chocolate or Strawberry Parfait....35	
Chilled Watermelon (In Season)....20	
Hot Fudge Sundae....35	

BEVERAGES

Coffee, cup ....10; pot 15	Buttermilk (bottle) 15
Milk (Individual Bottle)....10	Postum, pot 15
Half and Half, glass....25	Sanka 10
Cream, glass 35	Iced Lemonade 20
Orangeade 20	Iced Limeade 20
Coca-Cola 10	Iced Orangeade 20
7-Up 10	Hot Chocolate 10
Pepsi-Cola 10	Grapette 10
Root Beer 10	Milk Shake 20
Tea, pot 10	
Tearoom Special Malted Milk 25, with Egg or Ice Cream Floats 35	

TEA ROOM SHOWING OPEN·AIR PROMENADE

ide of the : with he distance

A Corner of the Home Like Foyer

guard: bankers, attorneys and businessmen, most with offices on Seventeenth Street, in the Equitable Building, the Boston Building, the Colorado National Bank and other landmarks of the "Wall Street of the West." While it is not possible today to trace any particular business deal to its being hatched in the Grill Room, having this many movers and shakers in one place every day likely contributed not only to feelings of camaraderie and connectedness but probably also to outsiders' perception, particularly in the early years after World War II, that Denver was very much in the control of a tight group of men who preferred their own company and ideas.[73]

Over time, the Tea Room evolved, as institutions will. In the 1940s and 1950s, a yellow canary named Bing greeted diners from his cage near the entrance. Denver artist Herndon Davis painted a series of portraits that were framed and hung around the room. They were of such Colorado luminaries and legends as mining millionaire Horace Austin Warner Tabor and his second wife, Baby Doe; showman William "Buffalo Bill" Cody; "Colorado Cannibal" Alfred Packer; scalawag Jefferson Randolph "Soapy" Smith; actor Douglas Fairbanks; actor Harold Lloyd; bandleader

The Grill Room round table in the 1940s or early 1950s. Western historian Fred Mazzulla stands fifth from left. Note the Herndon Davis paintings of famous Coloradoans on the columns. Governor Ralph L. Carr's portrait is visible at far right. *Linda Lebsack collection.*

Paul Whiteman; "Manassa Mauler" Jack Dempsey; railroad builder and banker David Moffat; Uncompaghre Ute chief Ouray and his wife, Chipeta; journalist and short story writer Damon Runyon; *Denver Post* co-owner Helen Bonfils; newsman Lowell Thomas; Denver mayors Robert Walter Speer and Benjamin Franklin Stapleton; and Governor Ralph Lawrence Carr, along with many others. In 1962, the Tea Room was closed for three weeks to allow for a complete kitchen remodeling, including installation of a two-ton dishwasher capable of handling nine thousand dishes and glasses daily, along with new paint and furnishings in the dining room. A 1976 redecorating in green and white led management to rename it the Greenhouse, a moniker it had first used for restaurant operations in suburban stores opened earlier that decade. In its final years, signage and menus bore the simple name The Denver Dry Goods Restaurant, although most patrons still called it simply "the tearoom." Also in the last decade of operations, the front part was subdivided, with a sixty-seat, limited-menu "Soup Kitchen" near the elevators providing a faster way to dine.[74]

Left: The Tea Room often hosted fashion shows, such as this one benefiting the East High School PTA in 1961. *Author's collection.*

Right: A late 1970s or early 1980s tearoom menu; note the store's "famous Chicken à la King" for $2.75. *Jim O'Hagan collection.*

The waitstaff was as legendary as the room itself, with long-term waiters and waitresses serving for twenty, thirty or more years. Longtime patrons became friends with the likes of Dorothy Howard Kenny, Katie Ganshaw, Elsa Reynolds, Maude Guyon, Loretta Saunders, Grace Brown, Louise Cohen, Helen Wagnon, Geraldine Luis, Agnes Graves, Al Fagardo and many others. It was a second home for most, with waitstaff bringing flowers grown in home gardens to grace the tables and calling it "the best place in the world to work." The waitstaff knew the customers, and the customers knew them. The kitchen crew was equally tenured, with Ray Kitchen, Milt Barratt, Dock Barnes and Fred Batchelor serving for decades.[75]

Thousands of Denver children attended special events at the Tea Room. Each November from 1926 to 1930, the store gave "dolls' tea parties," at which young girls, along with their favorite dolls from home, enjoyed cocoa served in miniature china cups and saucers (embossed with the store's name and now collectors' items). The first year about one thousand girls came, and at their peak, the parties attracted over three thousand; the only adults in the room were servers. Once the cocoa was consumed, along with more solid refreshments like cake and candy, a herald dressed

The 1927 Dolls' Tea Party commemorative cup from Japan's Noritake featured hand-painted flowers. *History Colorado Collection.*

in white satin tights announced the arrival of the purple-robed, pearl-adorned Fairy Princess, portrayed by Hazel Flowers Berndt, a store employee. She would welcome the children after strolling down a red carpet, her train held by another store employee acting as page. The princess would then invite the children to watch a play, *The Enchanted Garden*, at the Enchanted Castle set up at one end of the Tea Room. Other years' entertainments included a live band and a trained deer named Billy Colorado.[76]

Another young person's tradition was "Breakfast with Santa," held early on Saturday mornings in December. Children would arrive at the store with their parents (who, unlike at the dolls' tea parties,

This later (1950s–60s) view of the Tea Room shows closely placed tables for two. *Denver Public Library, Western History Collection, photograph by Morey J. Engle.*

were permitted to attend) and walk through the darkened first floor to the elevators. Upon arrival in the Tea Room, the youngsters would enjoy puppet shows, cartoons and other entertainments, along with a hearty breakfast, and then would get a chance to tell Santa Claus what they most wanted for Christmas. By the end of the breakfast, the store had opened for business, giving parents a chance to shop.[77]

Chicken à la King was the Tea Room's signature dish, at least in later decades; some early tearoom menus do not mention it. Salads were popular, as were standard sandwiches, such as the Reuben, smoked tongue on dark rye, sliced turkey breast or baked ham, tuna fish and roast beef. Heartier fare included pot roast with potato pancakes, prime rib of beef, Irish stew, liver with bacon or Baltimore oyster stew with fresh celery hearts. Signature soups included split pea, navy bean and vegetable beef. For dessert, diners could choose ice cream made in-house, various pies, rice or raisin pudding, peach cobbler, or bread pudding. Everything, until the final few years, was made from scratch (toward the end, most baking was done off-site).[78]

RECIPES

These six Tea Room recipes, including its famous Chicken à la King, were resized to domestic proportions from much larger Tea Room versions by the final executive chef, Fred Batchelor.[79]

Pecan Chicken Salad
Serves 8

3 pounds chicken meat, cooked, skinned and diced
2 ribs celery, diced
¼ cup pecans
1 medium red onion, sliced thin, then chopped
1 cup mayonnaise, thinned with ¼ cup water
1 teaspoon seasoned salt (or to taste)

Combine chicken, celery, pecans and onion. Gradually add enough of the mayonnaise mixture until ingredients are moist and lightly covered. Salt to taste.

Vegetable Beef Soup
Serves 8

2 quarts beef stock
¼ cup raw barley, washed
1 cup diced celery
1 cup diced carrots
½ cup diced onions
1 cup diced green pepper
1 bay leaf
1 cup peeled and diced potatoes
1 cup frozen cut corn
2 cups diced tomatoes
1 cup frozen cut green beans,
dash red pepper sauce
1 teaspoon Worcestershire sauce
¼ teaspoon thyme

salt to taste
pepper to taste
1 pound beef, cut into ½- by ¼-inch strips

Bring stock to a boil. Add barley and simmer for 1 hour. Add additional water to stock as it reduces to maintain ½-gallon quantity. Add celery, carrots, onions, pepper and bay leaf and simmer until vegetables are half done. Add all remaining ingredients, simmer ½ hour. Remove bay leaf and serve.

Navy Bean or Split Pea Soup
Serves 8

1 pound navy beans or lentils
¼ pound bacon, cut in small pieces
1 large onion, diced
3 ribs celery, diced
3 medium carrots, diced
1 clove garlic, minced
2 tablespoons flour
8 cups water
1 ham hock
½ teaspoon Worcestershire sauce
pinch sugar
salt and pepper to taste

Thoroughly wash beans or lentils. Soak navy beans overnight and drain. If lentils are used, it is not necessary to soak them. In soup kettle, sauté bacon with onion, celery, carrots and garlic. Blend in flour. Add about 4 cups of the water. Cook over moderate heat for about 10 minutes. Add remaining stock and ham hock. Simmer about 2 hours, or until beans are soft. Lentils will take less cooking time. Remove ham hock and pull meat from bones. Mince meat. Return to soup. Add more water if thinner soup is desired. Add Worcestershire sauce, sugar and salt and pepper. (Instead of ham hock, the Tea Room used ham stock, made with an intensely flavored paste with a ham base.)

Chicken à la King
Serves 8

2 sticks butter
1 ½ cups flour
8 cups chicken stock, or more (canned broth may be used)
1 cup half-and-half
1 pound cooked, skinless chicken meat, diced
1 large red bell pepper, cut in ¼-inch strips
1 large green bell pepper, cut in ¼-inch strips
½ pound sliced mushrooms, sautéed in butter
salt and white pepper to taste
baked puff pastry shells

Melt butter in large saucepan. Whisk in flour, cooking over moderate heat for a few minutes. Still whisking, gradually add chicken stock. Cook over moderate heat, whisking, until thickened. Whisk in half and half. Cook over low heat for about 25 minutes. Add more chicken stock, depending on desired consistency. Add remaining ingredients. Cook over low heat for about 20 minutes. Serve in pastry shells.

From a recipe book kept in the kitchen, the actual recipe for Chicken à la King, the Tea Room's signature dish, yielding six gallons. *Jim O'Hagan collection.*

Doc's Peach Cobbler
Serves 8

FILLING
1 cup packed brown sugar
5 teaspoons cornstarch
¼ teaspoon ground mace
¾ cup water
5 cups frozen peaches, thawed and sliced
1 tablespoon butter

PASTRY TOPPING
1¼ cups all-purpose flour
¼ teaspoon salt
⅓ cup shortening
3 to 4 tablespoons cold water

In a medium saucepan combine ¾ cup brown sugar, cornstarch and mace. Add ¾ cup water. Cook, stirring continuously until thick and bubbly. Add peaches and butter, and heat through. Pour into a greased 1½-quart casserole or 9- by 14-inch baking dish. Top with pastry topping and bake in a preheated oven at 400 degrees for 20 minutes. Top with remaining ¼ cup brown sugar. Let sit at room temperature 30 minutes before serving.

Pastry topping: In a mixing bowl combine flour and salt, mixing thoroughly. Cut in shortening until pieces are the size of peas. Sprinkle 1 tablespoon of cold water over part of flour mixture, toss with a fork. Continue adding water to the flour mixture until all the flour is moistened. Form into a ball.

Flatten the dough on a lightly floured surface with hands. Roll out from center to edge. Cut into ½-inch strips. Top the peach filling in a lattice pattern.

Bread Pudding
Serves 8

½ stick butter or margarine
8 slices white bread
¾ cup brown sugar
2 teaspoons cinnamon
¾ cup raisins
6 eggs, slightly beaten
½ cup granulated sugar
2 teaspoons vanilla
dash salt
6 cups milk, heated

Grease 9- by 12-inch pan with butter or margarine. Tear bread into pieces and let them fall in pan. Blend together remaining ingredients. Pour over bread. Bake, uncovered, in an oven preheated to 350 degrees for 45 minutes to 1 hour, or until knife inserted in center comes out clean.

A DENVER INSTITUTION

Our credo is both simple and strict. Every minute of every day The Denver Dry must be spotless, and every day we do something to improve its beauty, its service and its image....Fine stores like ours don't just happen.[80]

MODERNIZATION

The Denver Dry Goods Company, like most of the Mile High City's major stores, managed to survive the Great Depression and World War II, thanks to the careful financial management provided by Scruggs, Vandervoort and Barney and its local team. (The only major Denver store casualty of the Depression was A.T. Lewis and Son, which failed in early 1933.) But by the time the war ended, there was a sense that the postwar era required physical improvements and a new mindset. The first two decades after 1945 would bring significant changes to the store and its competitors, surviving legacies of the nineteenth century trying to remain relevant in a rapidly changing postwar world. The Denver was not alone in this: department stores around the nation were seeking ways to grow at a time when their customers were moving to new subdivisions ever farther away from city centers. While the 1950s, 1960s and 1970s would bring many new innovations in suburban shopping, the early postwar period saw most department stores reinvesting in their big downtown emporia to bring them up to date and foster easier shopping.[81]

At the end of World War II, yet another Irish American merchant, Charles A. Shinn, captained the store. A native of Mattoon, Illinois, he had become general manager in 1931, after twenty-five years of working at The Denver (his career began when he joined the silk department in 1906). He became president, succeeding Frank M. Mayfield, in 1944. Even before the war was over, Shinn announced that the postwar era would bring significant improvements, costing more than $1 million. He knew the deprivations of the Depression and war had created a pent-up demand for consumer goods, and he aimed to meet that demand. Assisting Shinn would be a Kansas native, Frank J. Johns, who had worked his way up through the store's drapery and home furnishings departments and who was Shinn's merchandise manager. (In 1948, Johns was elevated to the presidency, and Shinn to chairman of the board.) Together, Shinn and Johns would oversee a multi-decade era of continuous capital investments designed to keep the old store relevant to new generations of shoppers.[82]

The Denver Dry Goods, February 1947, poised for postwar growth. *History Colorado Collection.*

The first order of business was modernizing the building's internal transportation system. In 1947, the store ordered a completely new set of escalators from the Otis Elevator Company. Instead of just providing a one-way trip up to the second floor, the store's new stainless steel moving stairs (the old one had been of wood) would connect the first through the fourth floors, traveling both up and down. Costing $400,000, the new escalators were capable of carrying six thousand shoppers per hour, about the equivalent of ten elevators. Located in the Sixteenth Street building, they rose only to the fourth floor because to continue them to the fifth would have meant reducing the Tea Room's seating capacity. For reasons unknown, Shinn did not extend the escalators down to the basement bargain floor, although it is likely that the lower prices charged there affected his decision; bargain shoppers could still easily use stairs or take the elevators.[83]

A more significant improvement came in 1950, when the store opened its new "Fashion Floor" on two. While McNamara Dry Goods and the early Denver Dry Goods had been content to merchandise wares in a utilitarian way, the postwar era called for a more artistic approach. Consumers' expectations were higher. Not only did postwar prosperity create demand for higher-quality goods, but there was also a general sense that department stores should feel elegant, un-crowded and gracious. Shinn's answer was to spend significant sums of money ($425,000, or the equivalent of $3.39 million today) on the "biggest single project in The Denver Dry's history," nothing less than the complete reimagination of the entire second floor. Gone were views out the windows, Victorian iron columns and wooden floors. Instead, windows were hidden behind walls to allow for more dramatic vertical presentations and departmental signage, columns were encased in mirrored pillars and customers' feet could enjoy walking across "lush carpeting." Mannequins were grouped on raised platforms, and the entire floor featured a coordinated color scheme in pastel shades of mauve, rosewood and robin's egg blue. Second-floor departments included dresses, hats, shoes, coats, handbags and accessories, but the centerpiece was the new "Columbine Room," a salon for women to purchase better dresses in a leisurely setting. The Denver hired a fashion expert, Dorothy Miller, to run this new near-couture department, and she made it her mission to "never permit a woman to walk out of The Denver Dry Goods Company in a fashionable dress that didn't become her age, figure and type, or didn't compliment her silhouette, color, fabric and styling."[84]

Further renovations continued through the 1950s and into the 1960s, including installation of air conditioning in 1955 and remodeling the other

This circa 1958 window display in the corner at Sixteenth and California Streets featured Elizabeth Arden products on the shelves at left. *History Colorado Collection.*

floors to match the modern feeling of the second floor. The street floor was given a makeover in 1958, including a drop ceiling to allow for a completely new lighting system, which entailed a complete rewiring of the building to handle additional electrical load. The new lighting was "color-corrected fluorescent lights of the newest type," and the new ceiling was made up of square fiberglass panels hung from the original ceiling. Denver artist Reece Bolls executed wall decorations of pink and brown roses and stars, a series of bas-relief obelisks and, over the entrances, "the familiar Denver Dry Goods initial design…used by the store for years." The fourth floor, home to linens and domestics, among other departments, got its makeover in 1960, and the newly plush bargain basement, renamed the "Economy Floor," followed in 1962. The bargain department was located in the Sixteenth Street building; service-oriented departments, including the U.S. Post Office substation and shoe repair, occupied the basement on the Fifteenth Street side. As part of the remodeling, the store opened a snack bar on this floor, with those new jet-age wonders: automatic food and beverage vending machines (later, the snack bar was converted to a line-service operation).[85]

The Denver's postwar remodeling efforts are not yet evident in this 1950s Christmas scene on the first floor's main aisle; soon, it would be modernized with a new drop ceiling. *History Colorado Collection.*

This late 1960s view shows the store's efforts to beautify its exterior environment with potted trees. *Denver Public Library, Western History Collection, photograph by Sandra Dallas.*

By the mid-1960s, the downtown store was competing not just with the new May-D&F three blocks up Sixteenth at Tremont Street, with big ambitions to unseat The Denver as the leading Colorado retailer, but also with its own branches in the suburbs, with their much more modern buildings and acres of free parking. (The rollout of the branches is the subject of chapter 9.) Store president Frank Johns and his team did their best to keep "the old lady of California Street" (so christened by an otherwise flattering *Denver Post* article) sparkling, regularly repainting the store's exterior walls and sweeping the store's sidewalks daily, keeping them free from cigarette butts and other debris. The city's downtown booster organization made an attempt to beautify the shopping district by installing planters made of white cast stone, but as urban plantings will, they suffered from indifferent treatment. Not so on the sidewalks outside The Denver: the store filled these planters with thriving petunias, geraniums and small apple trees. The maintenance staff scrubbed the stone regularly to keep it white.[86]

Inside, 1965 saw the installation of a bright-red carpet runner down the length of the main aisle, and during the following year the store created new street floor departments to capture the attention of the rapidly maturing baby boom generation: Miss Denver for young women and mod men's clothing in "the Bailiwick." This new shop for "guys on the move" would be "a 'groovy' place featuring the NOW gear for young men imported from the brawly docks of London," one reporter wrote. Young Denver men yearning for a Carnaby Street Beatles look could now buy "turtle neck sweaters, high-collared print shirts with solid collar and cuffs, and slim wide-wale corduroy slacks with wide belts" at this old Victorian-era department store.[87]

BECOMING PART OF A LARGER FAMILY

In 1967, the store capped two decades of constant change and remodeling with a different kind of transformation: it decided to drop the words "Dry Goods" from its name, becoming instead what many Colorado shoppers had long been casually calling it: simply "The Denver." The exterior of the downtown store, which had long been painted a cream shade, was given a new coat of gleaming white, and the striped awnings sheltering the display windows were replaced with new "Columbine blue" awnings, part of a corporate branding effort that tied the store even more closely to Colorado tradition by utilizing the color of the official state flower (or something resembling it; the actual shade was closer to Wedgwood blue). The new cursive logo and blue-and-white color scheme graced shopping bags, wrapping paper, stationery, business cards and credit cards (still metal in those days and still called "charge-a-plates").[88]

This change of name, logo and color scheme came on the heels of another ownership change and may have been influenced by the new owners. The Denver had previously become a wholly owned subsidiary of Scruggs, Vandervoort and Barney in 1947 (its 1924 purchase of most of the stock had left a few independent shareholders), and in 1957, developer William Zeckendorf had flirted with the idea of buying the store to merge with Daniels and Fisher, which had already signed a lease to move to his

Courthouse Square project. He wanted fewer department stores downtown because he recognized that with the increasing suburbanization of shopping, there was going to be too much department store square footage in the city's core, and he needed his Courthouse Square tenant to succeed. He may have been using a potential Denver Dry Goods–Daniels and Fisher merger as a threat to May executives, with whom he was having difficulty negotiating. He knew that May desired greatly to become the largest store in the state, and if The Denver, instead of May, were to buy Daniels and Fisher, that could never happen. Zeckendorf even went so far as to purchase, in combination with Daniels and Fisher's then-parent Younker Brothers (a Des Moines, Iowa–based department store), 100,000 shares, or about 9 percent of the total, of Scruggs, Vandervoort and Barney stock, thereby becoming a partial owner, for a time, of The Denver. Zeckendorf, Younkers and May finally reached a deal, and May bought Daniels and Fisher in the fall of 1957. In August 1958, the old Daniels and Fisher and May stores closed, and the new May-D&F premiered at Courthouse Square. In a full-page newspaper advertisement that ran on May-D&F's opening day, The Denver welcomed "the new girl in town," pronouncing that what was good for downtown Denver was good for The Denver Dry Goods Company.[89]

In April 1964, the Marshall-Wells Company, a retail holding subsidiary of the Larchfield Corporation, announced it would purchase Scruggs, Vandervoort and Barney, and its subsidiaries, including The Denver Dry Goods. That purchase never took place. Instead, later that year store president Frank J. Johns, sensing that during a time when more and more retailers were consolidating, his store needed to become part of an organization larger than the relatively small Scruggs, approached Associated Dry Goods of New York City. He had known its president, Lewis P. Seiler, for some time. Associated and The Denver announced the transaction, which included only the Colorado-based store and not its St. Louis–based parent, in mid-December 1964, with the actual sale taking place the following March. The Denver was now part of a coast-to-coast operation that included J.W. Robinson (Los Angeles); Goldwater's (Phoenix); Stix, Baer & Fuller (St. Louis); Hahne and Company (Newark); Sibley's (Rochester, NY); and one of the nation's oldest department stores, Lord and Taylor of New York City (founded 1826). In coming years, Associated would provide The Denver with the financial strength to compete with May-D&F and Joslin's, and many of the store's new executives would hail from Associated's other divisions rather than being promoted from within.[90]

8

TRADITIONS

Wherever a bronco is being "busted," a calf being downed quickly or a quarter-miler going around the track, it is very likely the equipment has been furnished by The Denver Dry Goods Co.[91]

WESTERN OUTFITTERS TO THE NATION

The Denver was the only major Colorado store, and one of the few in the West, with a complete department to satisfy the needs of the professional cowboy and stockman.[92] Begun during the Sheedy years (remember that he had made his first fortune running cattle), the Western Shop, later christened the Stockmen's Store, was located on the fourth floor of the Fifteenth Street building (it later moved upstairs to the sixth). On the department wall, the store kept a large mural painted with the brands of the many hundreds of ranches it had served. Not only did The Denver sell clothing appropriate to the working cattleman—including canvas, denim, gabardine and leather garments, gloves and all manner of Stetson hats and Justin boots—but it also offered all kinds of necessary accessories, such as custom-fitted chaps, neckerchiefs and spurs. Women were not excluded; the store also kept women's versions of men's western wear in stock for those Denver metropolitan women who just wanted to dress up that way, perhaps for a barbecue or some public event, and for the women who worked in the cattle business.

The Stockmen's Store, on the fourth floor, circa 1948. *Denver Public Library, Western History Collection.*

For the stockman's best friend and workmate, his horse, the store offered its own line of saddles and tack, manufactured by a store subsidiary, the Powder River Saddlery (coincidentally located in the Granite Building, one-time home to McNamara Dry Goods). Sturdy saddles for everyday use were sold alongside much fancier hand-tooled models costing many hundreds of dollars (in Depression-era money). In 1945, the store added to the Powder River division by buying another longtime Denver saddler, the Herman H. Heiser Saddlery Company. Founded in 1859, when the city was less than a year old, the Heiser concern had its factory at 1424 Market Street (later relocated to 1089 Bannock Street) and was still run by Ewald F. Heiser, the son of the founder. The store kept the Heiser division for only five years, however, selling it in 1950 (but retaining the Powder River operation).

In addition to the department inside the store, The Denver also mailed out thousands of copies of its stockmen's catalogue, generating significant mail-order business. With the store billing itself "Western Outfitters to

The cover of the 1948–49 Stockmen's Store mail-order catalogue, "Western Outfitters to the Nation." *Linda Lebsack collection.*

the Nation," The Denver could brag that its customer base for western accoutrements spanned the entire United States and even foreign countries. The complete inventory was on offer in this catalogue, mailed twice each year, and included such additional gear as tents for camping and ropes for roping. Professional rodeo cowboys counted among the stores' clientele, as

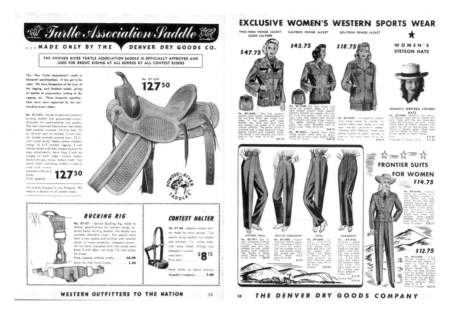

Two pages from the store's mail-order catalogue catering to working stockmen (and women): the store's signature Powder River saddles (*left*) and western wear for women (*right*). *Linda Lebsack collection.*

might be expected, but some of these distant Stockmen's Store customers were not rodeo stars or working cowboys at all; they were Hollywood movie stars featured in westerns, names (now remembered mostly by aficionados of the genre) such as Bill Hart, Ken Maynard and Harry Carey. Frank E. Newhagen oversaw the department during its peak years; later, it was under the management of W.J. Loeffler. The Stockmen's Store lasted through the 1950s, when western costumes and history were part of popular culture, but was gone by the 1970s.[93]

SATISFYING DENVER'S SWEET TOOTH

Another special department was the Sally Dee candy counter. Located on the first floor, the department sold 110 varieties of chocolates and other sugary sweets made by hand in the store's candy kitchen, upstairs in a corner of the sixth floor (Fifteenth Street building). The store had sold candies in a small way before the 1920s, but it was during that decade when Charles A. McFadden joined the store, took over the candy kitchen and built it into a popular feature of The Denver. He learned to make fudge (a big seller) from a nun, Sister Dorothy Ann Dunn of the Sisters of Loretto, taking her recipe and translating it into one that would produce much larger batches. Divinity and English toffee were also popular Sally Dee items, as were chocolate creams. All candies were made without preservatives so that customers could enjoy the freshest taste. About two-thirds were milk chocolate; Denver in those years was a "milk chocolate town," preferring milk to more intense dark chocolate. Over time, the candy kitchen added more employees, and by 1964, it was generating sales of $125,000 annually (the equivalent of about $955,000 today).[94]

FORTNIGHTS

In the early 1970s, the Denver engaged in what many other downtown stores across America were doing during that era to drive traffic to their big downtown flagships: it staged themed "fortnights" during the quieter time between the back-to-school and holiday shopping seasons. Department store fortnights, generally ten days to two weeks long, were usually based on a particular country or region, and buyers would import goods from that place to showcase its best offerings, often working with foreign governments' trade offices. During the fortnight, artists, artisans, craftspeople and performing artists would entertain shoppers with demonstrations and performances; newspapers gave these events ample publicity. The Denver's great rival in staging fortnights was May-D&F, which had begun holding them in 1960 on a biannual basis; although The Denver got started later, its events were just as memorable.

There were precedents. Beginning in 1947, every spring brought the annual Flower and Fragrance Show with Denver florists creating spectacular displays, each an interpretation of a famous perfume fragrance. In the spring of 1950, the store hosted a Dutch tulip show, with plants flown in from Holland; customers would place orders for bulbs that would arrive that fall for planting, dealing with sales ladies clad in traditional Dutch costumes, complete with kerchiefs and wooden shoes. Also in the 1950s, the store collaborated with the Denver Art Museum on displays of the museum's holdings (the museum was then housed in a Capitol Hill mansion, the Chappell House at 1300 Logan Street, with a small gallery annex at Thirteenth Avenue and Acoma Street). In 1958, the store partnered with *Holiday* magazine on a display of artwork from forty nations, including three—Romania, Poland and Czechoslovakia—from behind the Iron Curtain. These pieces, all of them representational rather than abstract, were meant to provide "a better understanding" of each country's "national life."[95]

The first true fortnight in 1970 would have pleased the heart of the store's founder Dennis Sheedy, of Michael J. McNamara before him and of later president Charles A. Shinn: an Irish exposition, dubbed "Irish Awakening." It may have been held in September, but it looked more like the seventeenth of March. For two weeks, shoppers could partake of all things Emerald Isle, from Donegal tweeds to Waterford crystal, from Belleek china to handwoven fabrics from the Kilkenny Design Workshop and from antique Irish silver to freshly made Irish soda bread. Children weren't left out; the third floor was home to Leprechaun Land, where the "wee ones" could hear tales told by an Irish storyteller and Irish bagpipes played. The Tea Room created a special Irish menu, with Guinness stout accompanying "hearty Irish fare."[96]

Patrick J. Lalor, Ireland's minister for industry and commerce, speaks to a gathered crowd at the opening of the Irish Awakening fortnight in 1970. Visible over his right shoulder is store president, W. Douglas Poole, and over his left, store special events director Rosemary Barnwell. *Author's collection.*

The following year, 1971, The Denver saluted its home state, with "Colorado—The Land of the Long Look," another event that Sheedy would have loved. The Centennial State festival highlighted "all of the state's cultural, educational, recreational, agricultural, industrial, commercial, environmental, and governmental development," like an old fashioned world's fair, but covering just one American state. The store collaborated with all sorts of institutions, public and private, on creating displays, including the Denver Convention and Visitors Bureau, National Jewish Hospital, National Center for Atmospheric Research, Adolph Coors Company, Denver Symphony Orchestra, Gates Rubber, Colorado Historical Society, Samsonite, Colorado Ski Country U.S.A., Mountain Bell, Colorado Public Lands Commission, Elitch Gardens amusement park and the 1976 Winter Olympics Committee (not yet made obsolete by the state's voters, who in 1972 killed the only Olympics ever awarded to Colorado). The festival opened with performances by the Air Force Academy Band and choral group Sing Out Colorado. Display windows featured exhibits of Martin-Marietta's outer space efforts, including Skylab and the Mars Landing Unit. Mountain Bell displayed a space-age communication device, the Video Phone. Scale models of the not-yet-built Chatfield Dam and Auraria Higher Education Center were also exhibited. Various departments sold Colorado-made goods (silver, candles, pottery and woven items) and hosted educational and promotional displays. The Tea Room served "down-to-earth food of the West."[97]

The next fortnight was an example of curious timing, to say the least. Coming just a few weeks after the 1972 Summer Olympics in Munich, West Germany, at which eleven Israeli athletes and one German doctor were taken prisoner and killed by the Palestinian terrorist group Black September, The Denver hosted a weeklong fair called "Shalom Shalom," in celebration of the twenty-fifth anniversary of modern Israel's founding and "echo[ing] Israel's good wishes for peace." The store announced it was sponsoring the planting of ten thousand trees in Israel, in "The Denver's Forest." A red mailbox borrowed from Tel Aviv gave shoppers an opportunity to send postcards to Israeli citizens, and the "Old City Bazaar" gave the flavor of a Jerusalem street, featuring small shops with craft items. On the first floor, water from the River Jordan and the Sea of Galilee filled temporary fountains, while Israeli fashion designers were featured in the Columbine Room on two. The Tea Room was included of course, with an area near the elevators set up to resemble the Old City of Jerusalem, complete with a white stone wall and a menu of traditional Jewish recipes.[98]

Denmark provided the theme for the September 1973 fortnight, "The Denver Salutes the Great Danes." A high-society benefit party for the Denver Symphony Orchestra in the Tea Room (done up as Copenhagen's famous Tivoli Gardens) launched the event, with Count and Countess Christian of Rosenborg as honored guests, as well as Denver's own Aksel Nielsen, a prominent businessman who had been knighted by King Christian IX. This event was more tailored to the theme country's high-fashion image than the Israeli event had been, with many clothing and jewelry designers flown in, but the arts of the ordinary Danish people were also well represented through crafts and folk dancers. The Danish Agricultural Marketing Board sent in the "Karoline Girls" to serve *Smørrebrød* (open faced sandwiches) in the Tea Room, while on the first floor representatives from the Danish Cheese Association handed out free samples of Danablu, Esrom, Mynster, Tybo, Fontina and Havarti in the Epicure Shop.[99]

Golden Age Greece provided the theme for the 1974 fortnight, held for two weeks beginning on September 15. The store collaborated with Denver's Hellenic Orthodox Cathedral and Olympic Airways in staging the event, and the kickoff party, again held in the Tea Room (decorated with Ionic columns and reproductions of Greek statuary), benefited that church. The store promoted Greek fashion designers (Tzanacakis, Calbari, Tseklenis) in the second-floor "Agora," and on the third floor, the furniture department featured an art show with Greek-themed works by Denver-area Greek American children. The Taverna (the Tea Room) served Greek soups, desserts and wines, and shoppers could take Greek delicacies home from Epicure on the first floor.[100]

After store president W. Douglas Poole (about whom there is more in chapter 10), who had been the driving force behind the fortnights, resigned in 1975, the expensive annual events were discontinued. This did not mean the end of special events in downtown and in some of the branches, but The Denver's new management, like that of May-D&F (which also had a new president at about this time), determined that the costs outweighed the benefits. After Greece, there would be no more fortnights until several years later, when The Denver hosted a festival of all things British. During "The Denver Salutes Great Britain," Alfie Howard, the official town crier of Lambeth, London, periodically strolled through the store with his fifteen-pound bell and booming voice, announcing events. These included Punch and Judy performances on the first floor; performances by a local troupe of actors, the Great City Combination, dressed up as London Bobbies, the British Beefeater and palace guards; and personal

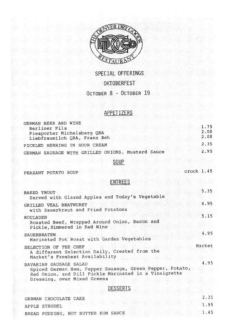

Left: The British fortnight included this special Tea Room menu, featuring food and beverages from the United Kingdom. *Jim O'Hagan collection.*

Right: The Tea Room celebrated Oktoberfest with a special menu in the early 1980s. *Jim O'Hagan collection.*

appearances by Michael Doulton, who would autograph purchased pieces of Royal Doulton chinaware. The Denby and Wedgwood firms also sent special pieces of their china. The third floor was especially British, with a "Kings and Queens of England" exhibit, English antique shops and model rooms showing life in the English countryside, a gentleman's London flat and a Scottish summer cottage. The book department featured newspapers and magazines flown in from the United Kingdom. Upstairs on four, the housewares department sold English marmalades, jams, chutneys, pickles, cookies, crackers and teas. As usual, the Tea Room was part of the show, with a special British menu of Welsh rarebit (rabbit), fish and chips, steak and mushroom pie and British beers.[101]

In 1982 there was one last hurrah, an event called "Voyage of Discovery: The Arts and Crafts of China." Unlike the earlier fortnights, this was not exclusive to downtown but was also celebrated at the Southglenn, Cherry Creek and Cinderella City branches. The emphasis was on Chinese craftsmanship, and several artisans from the People's Republic of China were on hand for demonstrations, including dough artists, paper-cut masters, painters, enamel workers and flower arrangers. The store's buyers worked to bring in many items for sale that a typical American tourist to China would not be able to find, and goods ranged from carved chopsticks ($2 to $5) to elaborate kites designed to resemble birds in flight ($139), as well as a carved turquoise sculpture for $19,150. Voyage of Discovery also included a photography exhibit by the Denver Museum of Natural History's Charles T. Crockett and Robert Wright.[102]

HOLIDAYS

As the city's leading department store, The Denver Dry Goods, from its founding until the winter before it closed, always celebrated the December holidays in a big way. Newspaper advertisements were filled with images of Christmas, along with gift ideas for everyone in the family from the youngest

For the 1938 Christmas season, the store's windows celebrated the great diversity of ways to mark "Christmas in America." This Minnesota Scandinavian Christmas diorama is bracketed by "trees" of ribbons decked out with twenty-nine-cent embroidered handkerchiefs. *History Colorado Collection.*

Left: A 1902 mail-order catalogue page featured a game celebrating Theodore Roosevelt's Rough Riders, along with all sorts of other Christmas gifts for girls and boys. *Jim O'Hagan collection.*

Below: Exactly which year The Denver began hanging its Christmas chandeliers along the four-hundred-foot first-floor main aisle is unknown, but the tradition continued until the final holiday season in 1986. Every year brought a different theme and color scheme; this scene is probably from the late 1960s. *History Colorado Collection.*

to the oldest. In the years after World War II, the store chose to celebrate in a more religious way than it had done before the war or would do later; a 1955 Nativity crèche filled the main window at Sixteenth and California Streets, and in 1958, a newspaper advertisement featured the lyrics to "Happy Birthday," with "Dear Christ Child" named in the third line, along with a biblical quotation.[103]

Holiday decorations set the mood for serious shopping. The first floor downtown was especially festive, with the four-hundred-foot main aisle hung with a long row of spectacular chandeliers, installed just for the season and taken down after January's National Western Stock Show (city boosters used to encourage merchants to keep holiday lights up to impress visitors in town for that annual event). Every year, the chandeliers' trimmings would change to match the store's chosen holiday theme, everything from angels to teddy bears, but they always made the store feel like the most Christmas-y spot in town. While The Denver was not known for animated show windows (as May-D&F

was), its holiday displays were no less interesting, with merchandise surrounded by lush trimmings, often coordinated to tell a story. Even during the store's final years, when the Sixteenth Street flagship's operating costs were making it unprofitable, the store's director of visual merchandising, Gerald J. Greenwood, made sure that people venturing downtown to see the windows would not go away disappointed. He crafted a series of memorable themes, including Dickens's *A Christmas Carol*, "Christmas in France" and "A Neapolitan Christmas."[104]

Santa Claus was always present, of course. Not only could children sit on his lap and list what they wanted, both downtown and in the suburban stores (somehow he magically got around to all of

Employees were not forgotten during the busy holiday season; this Christmas Bonus Folder is from the 1950s, and the inside features printed signatures of Charles A. Shinn, Frank J. Johns and other executives. *Linda Lebsack collection.*

In 1983, Sixteenth Street windows portrayed Charles Dickens's *A Christmas Carol*, with Ebeneezer Scrooge confronting the Ghost of Christmas Past (*above*) and Bob Cratchit returning home with Tiny Tim on his shoulder (*below*). *Photographs by author.*

them), but he also made appearances at the annual breakfasts with Santa in the Tea Room, as described in chapter 6. Male store executives and managers, especially those with "older" voices, were conscripted to man a phone bank on Sunday evenings in December, from 5:00 to 7:00 p.m. Parents would dial a special number, and children would talk live on the phone to the red-suited elf from the North Pole. The men who took the calls had a great time and remember them fondly.[105]

BRANCHING OUT

The moment you step inside the doors you'll see an exciting "new look" everywhere…in the dynamic design and décor of the building and fixtures…in the fine fashions and wonderful wares. You'll marvel at the complete comfort of the modern air conditioning; you'll delight at the convenience of the large, free parking area.[106]

DECENTRALIZING THE DEPARTMENT STORE

With the end of World War II in 1945, the United States was about to enter a sustained period of prosperity. America alone of the major powers had come out of the war not only without having sustained damage to its industries but also with greater economic power, setting it up for several decades of unprecedented growth. After an initial postwar period of economic uncertainty, by the end of the 1940s, the economy began building up steam. Consumer goods became ever more plentiful and affordable, and a great middle class was buying cars and comfortable homes in new, low-density suburbs. Patterns were changing, and department stores, knowing they had to follow their customers or suffer the consequences, began to evolve away from the old model of massive downtown emporia.

This was not entirely a postwar phenomenon. As early as the 1920s, some stores (although none in Colorado) began experimenting with suburban branches to combat the rise of national chains like Sears, Roebuck and Montgomery Ward that were opening stores away from downtowns, closer to where people lived and cheaper to build thanks to lower land costs outside city centers. Early pioneers in branch development tended to open boutiques rather than full-line department stores. These included Boston's Filene's, which opened branches near college campuses, catering to female students; San Francisco's I. Magnin, which opened shops at fashionable California resort hotels; and New York's Saks Fifth Avenue, which had a program similar to Magnin's but spread farther afield, all the way to southern Florida. The pattern that would be picked up nationally after World War II was set by Chicago's Marshall Field & Company, which followed its big-spending customers to the city's own suburbs, opening larger branches, with all downtown departments represented, in Lake Forest, Evanston and Oak Park. Although the Great Depression and World War II put a halt to most suburban department store development, those years saw Bullock's of Los Angeles open an iconic suburban store on Wilshire Boulevard in 1929, followed by May Company in 1938–39. The May store proved that heavy pedestrian traffic, typical of downtown shopping streets, was unnecessary for success; it also demonstrated that suburban branches could be very large (in May's case, 270,000 square feet) and that customers would flock to a store with ample free parking.[107]

After the war, it was time for regional stores like The Denver to capitalize on the precedents set by the nascent branches of prewar decades. The new suburban stores would not only offer plentiful free parking but also a new, more casual relationship with the customer. She need no longer get formally dressed up (dress, stockings, gloves and hat) and deal with the logistical hurdles of a trip downtown with small children in-tow but could stop in on a whim, picking up a new blouse or a lamp for the spare bedroom on her way to fetch the children from school. With the wartime female workforce sent back to the domestic hearth to free up jobs for returning servicemen, middle-class women had more leisure time and, thanks to postwar prosperity, the means to become good American consumers. Department stores readied themselves.

THE 1950s: INITIAL FORAYS

The Denver always proudly called itself a "store of firsts," and it was first here, too, opening the earliest suburban department store branch in Colorado.[108] To call its first branch "suburban," however, is a misnomer, as it was located well inside Denver city limits, at East First Avenue and University Boulevard, less than four miles from downtown. Store president Frank Johns made the announcement at an all-employee breakfast just before Thanksgiving 1950. The branch, located adjacent to the Denver Country Club, would anchor a new shopping center, initially sporting the ungainly name "Coloden Moor," to be built by the Buell Development Corporation. Wisely, before the center opened in 1953, it would be rechristened "Cherry Creek," named for the stream that bordered it on the south.

The center's developer, Temple Hoyne Buell, was a Denver fixture. Born in Chicago in 1895, Buell had suffered a phosgene gas attack in France during World War I and, developing tuberculosis after his return, came to Denver to recover his health. He remained in the Mile High City for the rest of his long life. Already possessing a master's degree in architecture and married to a wealthy Chicago socialite, Buell bought the land (then a refuse dump) that would become Cherry Creek Shopping Center in 1925 with no concrete plans in mind. He made his mark architecturally with a series of highly visible commissions, including the Paramount Theater on Glenarm Place downtown, the State Services Building on East Colfax Avenue opposite the capitol, and twenty-six schools, among them Horace Mann Junior High, Merrill Junior High and Abraham Lincoln High. A canny businessman, he managed just fine during the Great Depression, until his firm grew into one of the largest architectural practices in Denver.[109]

During the years between Buell's purchase of the dump in 1925 and the war's end in 1945, department stores and property developers had experimented with various ways of combining multiple shops into a new type of development called "shopping centers." The first, begun by Kansas City residential developer J.C. Nichols in 1922, was that city's Country Club Plaza, a series of aesthetically pleasing buildings with close-at-hand free parking, tenanted by better shops that catered to the buyers of his nearby luxury homes. According to architectural historian Richard Longstreth, Nichols's motivation was to provide controlled commercial development that would enhance neighboring residential property values, in contrast to the typical unplanned arterial strips he considered not only ugly but also detrimental to nearby homeowners who had no say in what got built. A few other centers (some with small department store branches) opened in the 1920s and 1930s, but the full-blown shopping center concept, anchored by a department store and boasting substantial parking, did not really emerge in a big way until after World War II. Many of those first postwar centers, called "regional malls" (not yet fully enclosed), were often built not by

The Temple Buell–designed Cherry Creek store, facing University Boulevard, featured modern lines in keeping with the spirit of the times, circa 1953. *Denver Public Library, Western History Collection.*

developers but by the department stores themselves; controlling the entire center, they could ensure that smaller tenants complemented their offerings and would not provide too much direct competition. Early examples of department store–built centers included Bellevue Square, developed by Seattle's Frederick & Nelson in 1945–46, and Broadway-Crenshaw Center in Los Angeles, built by the Broadway department store in 1946–47. Some adventurous commercial developers did build centers early after the war, however, most notably Huston Rawls, who created the Jordan Marsh–anchored Shopper's World in Framingham, Massachusetts, in 1951.[110] Most Denver retailers were unwilling to take the financial risk of developing their own centers; except for May Company (which developed or codeveloped centers at University Hills in southeast Denver and Westland in Lakewood), they would leave shopping center development to real estate professionals. But like their center-developing peers, they would insist on being the sole anchor until examples in other cities demonstrated that having two department stores in one venue could increase business for both.

For the city's first department store–anchored shopping center, Buell envisioned a two-story department store near University Boulevard with an open-air landscaped mall running eastward from it, flanked by several one-story buildings that would house branches of local and national chain stores and restaurants. This would be surrounded on all sides by approximately 1,500 parking spaces. With Buell owning land stretching east to Steele Street, Cherry Creek would be built in stages, as business conditions warranted, similar to the model set by J.C. Nichols in Kansas City. Initially intending to use structural steel, Buell modified his design to utilize reinforced concrete due to a postwar National Production Authority limitation on steel that was still in effect in the early 1950s. The final version of the department store enveloped 92,600 square feet of space in a distinctly modern, clean-lined building faced with blond brick. On the main floor, thick limestone pillars divided the display windows, which were adjacent to entrances on the west, north and east (mall-facing) sides of the building. The windowless second floor and basement provided the store enough space to house all of the usual departments.

To create the most modern facility possible, Johns and board chairman Charles A. Shinn toured new branch stores popping up in other cities. Air conditioning was a must, of course, as were escalators connecting all levels (which were also served by an elevator). The second-floor carpet ran wall to wall, providing quiet acoustics, and both fluorescent and incandescent fixtures, including adjustable spotlights to highlight mannequins, allowed for lighting flexibility. Another innovation was music played over the store's public address system. Fixtures were built of steel and glass, as well as exotic woods, including Sapele mahogany, polished birch, African rosewood, antiqued oak and wormy chestnut. (Dennis Sheedy, whose home featured different woods in every room, would have enjoyed this aspect.) Individual departments were given their own color schemes, allowing customers to "read" the store at a glance, but the various shades harmonized well. The store was organized logically, with the basement (called the "Lower Main Floor" because "basement" didn't connote luxury) home to more prosaic departments, such as furniture, floor coverings, linens and lamps, along with luggage, records, radio and television. The first floor (Street Level) included women's accessories, cosmetics and jewelry, along with men's departments, books, cameras, baked goods and Sally Dee candies. Upstairs, shoppers found all of the ladies' clothing departments, along with children's and infants' wear. To staff the store, The Denver hired some new people but also transferred many from downtown so regular customers would find familiar faces. Currying the favor of Denver's upper crust, the store recruited volunteers from the Junior League to model designer clothing during the grand opening weekend.

Society women loved the store, located as it was not only near the Country Club neighborhood but also just a quick drive down University Boulevard from Cherry Hills Village, Denver's most affluent suburb (where Buell himself lived and in which he had had a hand developing). Denver's middle-class women embraced it, too, so that by the store's first anniversary in 1954, Johns could report that it had beaten their most optimistic financial projections, generating income in the first year comparable to what he had expected for the store's second year. Buell's shopping center proved popular as well and quickly filled up; he had other buildings ready on his drawing board, and he soon built them. Sears, Roebuck was so impressed by The Denver's success that it moved its downtown store (on Broadway near Seventeenth Avenue) to a site across First Avenue from Buell's project. The Denver's downtown rival Neusteter's followed in 1960, building a four-level store at First Avenue and Milwaukee Street. Temple Buell knew when he

The Cherry Creek Shopping Center's promenade, anchored by The Denver Dry Goods at its western end, featured a mixture of local (Fontius Shoes, Baur's restaurant) and national (F.W. Woolworth) tenants, circa 1953. *Denver Public Library, Western History Collection.*

bought the old dump in 1925 that the area had commercial potential due to its proximity to well-heeled Denverites; by the time of his 1990 death, the Cherry Creek district had become the city's primary shopping area, superseding downtown.

With the needs of southeastern neighborhoods well met by Cherry Creek, The Denver next decided to build a store for northwestern suburbs. In 1908, the town of Lakeside had been incorporated so that an amusement park, "Lakeside, the White City," could serve beer to its patrons. Lakeside's land, just west of Sheridan Boulevard between West Forty-Fourth and Forty-Eighth Avenues, was adjacent to a Denver neighborhood called Berkeley, a former incorporated town that a few years earlier had allowed itself to be annexed to Denver with the proviso that it be allowed to remain "dry," with no alcohol permitted. The Lakeside men feared that if their amusement park were to be annexed by Denver it might fall under Berkeley's alcoholic ban, so to avoid that fate, they established an independent town. Lakeside's western boundary was Harlan Street, and while the amusement park fronted on Sheridan, the town's southwestern corner, separated from the park by

An aerial view of Lakeside Shopping Center looking southeast toward downtown, circa 1960, after Montgomery Ward (right) joined The Denver (center of mall) as an anchor. *Linda Lebsack collection.*

An aerial view of Lakeside looking northeast toward Lakeside Amusement Park and Speedway, circa 1956. *Linda Lebsack collection.*

the eponymous lake (originally Lakeside Lake, now Lake Rhoda), remained undeveloped. Given the "wet" orientation of the town's founders, it was ironic that the man who bought this land to develop a shopping center in the 1950s was an avowed enemy of alcohol, so much so that his leases included a clause forbidding its sale. Gerri Von Frellick, an Oklahoma-born Baptist, had arrived in Denver in 1952 with only a two-dollar bill to his name after overextending himself building commercial properties in Texas. He would soon become one of Colorado's best-known shopping center builders.

In March 1955, Von Frellick announced "Lakeside Shopping City" (later renamed Lakeside Mall) to be anchored by a branch of The Denver Dry Goods that would be, at 130,000 square feet, about 25 percent larger than the Cherry Creek store. Similar to Cherry Creek, the store would be joined by other shops (both national and local); the main approach to the store would be via a landscaped, open-air mall; and the center would boast ample free parking. Construction began immediately, and the center, about four miles northwest of downtown Denver, was complete by the late summer of 1956. Visitors to The Denver's grand opening on August 29 could enter the store in two ways: the basement "Lake Level," with an entry facing north toward Lake Rhoda, or the "Mall Level," whose entry faced south toward West Forty-Fourth Avenue. There was also an "Upper Level." The Lakeside store was organized very much like Cherry Creek, with the Lake Level featuring home-related departments, along with a Stockmen's Store to cater to the "horsey set" living in the then semirural area west of Lakeside. The Mall Level housed ladies' cosmetics and accessories along with menswear, and the Upper Level was home to "better" and "budget" dresses, millinery, children's clothing and toys. The Denver was initially joined by coanchors W.T. Grant and Company and White's Stores (both considered "junior" department stores, and thus not a serious threat to The Denver), along with a King Soopers grocery store. Later, Montgomery Ward built a branch at the mall western end, and in the 1970s, Target became an anchor on the east when the center was converted into an entirely enclosed mall. These other anchors were more budget-oriented than The Denver, making it the most upscale store at Lakeside.[111]

THE 1960s: FARTHER AFIELD

After opening Cherry Creek and Lakeside, The Denver would wait another dozen years before opening any more branches in the immediate Denver metropolitan area. In 1968, it opened two branches in quick succession.

First up was a branch in another Gerri Von Frellick project, the one for which he is best remembered: Cinderella City.[112] (After Lakeside and before Cinderella City, he had also built the Villa Italia mall in Lakewood, but that center had Joslin's, rather than The Denver, as its locally based anchor.) As early as 1961, The Denver was set to be a tenant for Cinderella City, originally proposed for a fifty-six-acre site on the northwest corner of South University Boulevard and East Hampden Avenue. The land was home to radio station KLZ's transmitter, and the station's then-owner, Time Inc., would have been a development partner. The first Cinderella City never got off the drawing board, however, due to strong opposition from nearby residential areas (including many in adjacent Cherry Hills Village, where rival developer Temple Buell lived) that turned into a series of court cases and a municipal election. The KLZ land had been annexed by Englewood, and not wanting to forego the potential sales tax revenues Cinderella City might generate, in 1964 the city's politicians and business leaders came up with a new proposal. Englewood would sell to Von Frellick its main public park, located along West Hampden Avenue near South Santa Fe Drive. The developer would combine it with an adjacent nine-hole golf course to create a sixty-one-acre plot. This plan also met with opposition, mostly from citizens upset over the loss of the park and property owners living very near it. They pursued their case to the Colorado Supreme Court (which voted seven to zero in favor of the shopping center) and seriously considered appealing to the U.S. Supreme Court, but not having the budget to do so, they gave up. By late 1965, all legal obstacles were out of the way.

The second Cinderella City would officially bear the name "New Englewood Shopping Center: Cinderella City," although Von Frellick dropped "New Englewood" not long after opening. At 1.6 million square feet, Cinderella City was one of the largest malls in the nation on its March 7, 1968 debut and boasted over seven thousand parking spaces on two levels. The enclosed mall's floor plan, designed to accommodate over 250 stores, was unorthodox: a W-shaped layout that required a very long hike to get from one end to the other. The main anchor stores featured three levels, which opened to lower-level malls as well as the main floor. The Denver, with 151,000 square feet (about 75 percent larger than Cherry Creek), had as coanchors similarly large J.C. Penney and Joslin's stores, along with the departmentalized specialty stores Neusteter's and Gano-Downs. The Denver and J.C. Penney fronted on a dramatic two-level central atrium, the Blue Room, which featured a 20-foot-high fountain and lush tropical plants. The vast mall was an instant sensation upon opening, attracting business from a wide swath of the southern Denver metro area and foothills.

The Denver opened its second new store of 1968 just a week after Cinderella City, on the northern suburban fringe at a new center, the fully enclosed ("climate-controlled" in the parlance of the day) Northglenn Mall. Located in Adams County, Northglenn (originally North Glenn) was a Colorado version of Levittown, the inexpensive suburbs of New York City and Philadelphia that had sprung up in the post–World War II building boom. Begun by Perl-Mack Enterprises (whose principals were Jordan Perlmutter, Samuel Primack and William S. Morrison) in 1959, the young Northglenn, centered on 104th Avenue eleven miles north of downtown Denver, had grown from zero to over ten thousand residents in only three years, and had been named "America's Most Perfectly Planned Community" by *Life* magazine in 1963. To serve Northglenn's burgeoning population, Perl-Mack developed an 800,000-square-foot center, Northglenn Mall, which opened at 104th Avenue and Interstate 25 on March 14, 1968. The 139,000-square-

The Cinderella City store opened in 1968. Its exterior is shown here circa 1979. *History Colorado Collection.*

A postcard of the interior view of the Cinderella City store across the "Blue Room" toward The Denver, circa 1970. *Author's collection.*

foot branch of The Denver was joined by anchors J.C. Penney and Sears and would draw customers from Northglenn, Thornton, Westminster, Broomfield, Longmont and Brighton.[113]

In addition to the two Denver-area branch stores, the 1960s also saw The Denver extend its reach beyond the metropolitan area. It had long conducted a mail-order business, and customers across Colorado and the Rocky Mountain West were well acquainted with the store's reputation for quality and service. In June 1962, Greeley Grows Greater Inc., a city-boosting organization in that Weld County seat that was home to Colorado State College (now University of Northern Colorado) and a large meatpacking plant, inked a deal with The Denver Dry Goods. Greeley Grows Greater bought the land at Eighth Avenue and Eighth Street, demolished a former post office and built a structure to house the big-city store. The new branch, fifty miles north of downtown Denver, occupied forty-eight thousand square feet on two levels and was a full-line store with the usual departments, including a Stockmen's Store to cater to farmers and ranchers who lived nearby. The Greeley store opened in August 1963.[114]

Crossroads Mall in Boulder was announced the same year, 1962, that The Denver decided to open its Greeley branch, but initially, The Denver would not be an anchor. Yet another Gerri Von Frellick project, Crossroads initially signed up Montgomery Ward and J.C. Penney, but no local department stores, as primary anchors for the mall located on Twenty-Eighth Street and

The Northglenn Mall store opened in 1968, photograph circa 1979. *History Colorado Collection.*

The downtown Greeley store opened in 1962, photograph circa 1979. *History Colorado Collection.*

The Crossroads Mall store in Boulder opened in 1963 as the Randall Shop and expanded in 1976 to become The Denver, photograph circa 1979. *History Colorado Collection.*

Arapahoe Avenue, on the then-eastern edge of Boulder near the University of Colorado campus. In February 1963, however, The Denver announced it would open a small branch, occupying ten thousand square feet. This would not be a full-line store but a clothing-only facility christened "Randall Shop," a name it had originally used for a satellite it had opened near the campus three decades earlier (not unlike the Filene's branches opened around Boston-area colleges, discussed previously). By naming it "Randall Shop," there was no promise of a full department store experience, but the lease included a provision that the store could eventually expand to sixty thousand square feet, allowing for more departments in the future. For more than a decade, Boulderites had to be content with the Randall Shop, but March 1976 saw the opening of a "full-fashion" store (sans furniture department) with The Denver's name on it. The Denver gutted its space and took over adjacent parts of the mall to build an entirely new store five times larger (fifty-two thousand square feet), all on one level.[115]

THE 1970s AND 1980s: COVERING THE MAP AND BEYOND

The Denver announced its next metropolitan branch in 1972. Having had success at the developer's Northglenn Mall, it entered into an agreement with Perl-Mack Companies to anchor Southglenn Mall, at South University Boulevard and East Arapahoe Road in unincorporated Arapahoe County (today included in the city of Centennial, incorporated in 2001). For the first time in the metro area, The Denver would be paired with its primary rival, May-D&F, as anchors; Sears would join them. Southglenn opened on August 15, 1974, and proved an immediate hit. The Denver had always called itself the "store of firsts," and at Southglenn it had another: the first Denver department store branch managed by a woman, Marie Salman. Transferred from the Randall Shop in Boulder, Salman would oversee more than two hundred employees and eighteen departments in a two-level (May-D&F and Sears each had only one floor), 123,000-square-foot store that would cater to affluent suburbanites who had formerly driven several miles north to Cherry Creek. The new store, with a dramatic arched colonnade sheltering its parking lot entrance, featured its own tearoom, a plant-filled refuge overlooking the mall's center court dubbed the "Greenhouse." Managed by Evelyn Klug, who had previously managed the clubhouse at

The Southglenn Mall store opened in 1974, photograph circa 1979. *History Colorado Collection.*

Cherry Hills Country Club, the Southglenn store's restaurant was the first suburban food service operation for The Denver and the first to feature cocktails, wine and beer. A dramatic glass elevator, another first for a Denver department store, connected the two levels.[116]

A year later, 1975 saw the opening of another large branch, this one on the metropolitan area's eastern fringe. Aurora Mall, second only to Cinderella City in size within Colorado, opened on August 14 of that year. As at Southglenn, The Denver competed with its closest rival, May-D&F, this time facing each other across a central two-level atrium; J.C. Penney and Sears joined them at opposite ends. The site, at East Alameda Avenue and Interstate 225, sloped down from southwest to northeast, which allowed the anchors entrances on both levels. The Denver's 120,000-square-foot store, built of dark-brown brick (brown had become the store's signature color in a recent graphics overhaul), featured dramatic steel and glass canopies over its entrances and, like Southglenn, included a food service operation named the Greenhouse, along with a high-fashion Columbine Room and Canned Ego beauty salon. Although Aurora at this time was still relatively undeveloped east of Interstate 225, the mall provided an impetus to builders, and Aurora Mall was soon surrounded by subdivisions on all sides. The Denver occupied the prime spot, easily visible from the freeway.[117]

The 1970s also saw The Denver again open branches at some distance from the metropolitan area. Store executives envisioned a chain that would dominate the department store trade not only immediately around Denver but also along the entire Front Range and made bold moves that were sometimes successful, sometimes not. Colorado Springs, an hour south of Denver, would see the first of these far-flung branches. Development of the Citadel, a two-level mall anchored by a 110,000-square-foot branch of The Denver and a large J.C. Penney, at Academy Boulevard and U.S. Highway 24, began in 1968, and the center opened its doors on a frigid February morning in 1972. A comparable distance in the opposite direction, Fort Collins would be next. This was similar to the Boulder Crossroads store, in that it had begun life as a limited-range Randall Shop close to the Colorado State University campus. But instead of opening another boutique in the new Foothills Fashion Mall, The Denver would open a full-fashion (furniture excluded) department store, one of three anchors alongside Sears and May-D&F. This was the same trio as at Southglenn, and The Denver opened in August 1973.

The Aurora Mall store opened in 1975, with entrances on both levels, photograph circa 1979. *History Colorado Collection.*

The Citadel store in Colorado Springs opened in 1972, photograph circa 1979. *History Colorado Collection.*

The Foothills Fashion Mall store in Fort Collins opened in 1973, photograph circa 1979. *History Colorado Collection.*

The last two new stores of the 1970s, both announced in January 1978, would open even farther away from the store's namesake city. The 60,000-square-foot, single-level Billings, Montana store, in that city's Rimrock Mall, opened in the fall of that year, and it was followed about a year later by a 53,500-square-foot store in the Pueblo Mall in Pueblo, Colorado. Although these were not large stores, The Denver made sure every department except furniture had representation. But while the chain could now boast eleven locations, and a geographic reach that stretched more than 650 miles north to south, these final two branches of the 1970s made little sense from a marketing perspective. Neither Billings nor Pueblo could boast large concentrations of the sorts of shoppers that had made the

The Southwest Plaza store (left), probably just before opening in 1983. *Denver Public Library, Western History Collection.*

store so successful in Denver and its suburbs, and both were far enough from the city that the store's name didn't resonate with shoppers the way it did even with citizens of Colorado Springs or Fort Collins. Neither store would remain open very long.

The final branch of The Denver to open would be one of five anchors for the last retail project of Perl-Mack Companies (creators of the earlier Northglenn and Southglenn Malls): Southwest Plaza. Located, as its name implies, in the southwestern suburbs of Denver at South Wadsworth Boulevard and West Bowles Avenue, Southwest Plaza would be upon opening the second-largest mall in the Denver area after Cinderella City and would serve residents of vast new subdivisions that hadn't existed ten years earlier. With The Denver joined by May-D&F, Joslin's, J.C. Penney and Sears, the new mall opened with great fanfare in March 1983. By this time, new leaders had replaced the management team that had green-lighted the ill-considered expansions into Billings and Pueblo. These new men (about whom, see the next chapter) had restored The Denver's position as the most upscale of the city's full-line department stores, and for Southwest Plaza, they created what was arguably the most elegant of all of The Denver's branches. A large escalator atrium connected the two levels, and for one mirrored wall between the floors, they commissioned Santa Fe artist Frank Howell to create a signature triptych painting, *Spirit of the West*, that measured six feet high by ten feet wide and served as the visual anchor for a store that featured warm earth tones and aisles paved in brown Mexican "Café Goleta" marble tiles. This most elegant of all of The Denver's branches would serve its customers for only four years.

10

POSTWAR DECADES

We have a heritage that we are the preferred store. I am formulating plans to become the dominant store in the trading area.[118]

THE STORE AND ITS EMPLOYEES

For all the energy spent over the years to open The Denver's branches, the downtown flagship remained the paramount symbol of the company, and during the decades after World War II, it became the focus of efforts by social justice activists.

After the war, employee relations were seemingly as good as they always had been. A vestige of the 1902 dress code remained in place, with employees expected to dress conservatively so as not to appear "showy," although this would finally be relaxed in the 1960s and 1970s. While the store had continued to pay according to prevailing Denver retail workers' wages (see chapter 4), in the late 1940s, postwar inflation had begun taking a severe toll on all wage earners' abilities to live decently, and The Denver's clerks were not immune. In the late summer of 1946, workers at May Company had gone on strike, picketing at the corner of Sixteenth and Champa Streets all through the holidays and into the following spring, when labor and management finally reached an agreement.[119]

In 1947, with May Company clerks having shown it could be done, it was The Denver Dry Goods workers' turn to press for better wages. In August, the National Labor Relations Board (NLRB) ordered an election for the store's workers after Local 454 of the Retail Clerks Union of the American Federation of Labor (AF of L, the same local that represented May staffers) had begun organizing employees. The vote was held in mid-November, and with over 800 workers casting ballots, the pro-union side won, 410 to 394. At the same time, workers at the company's warehouse voted to join the Teamsters' Union (AF of L) by a more lopsided margin, 21 votes for to 2 against. It should be remembered that the Taft-Hartley Act, which greatly restricted the activities of unions, had passed Congress and had become effective the previous June; President Harry S Truman had vetoed it, but Congress overrode his decision. One provision of the act was that "sympathy" strikes by parties not directly involved in a business were outlawed; the AF of L's threat of such a general strike had been an important tool for the union during the May Company dispute that it could no longer use.

The local immediately began negotiations with management for better wages under a storewide contract but made little progress. By July 1948, after eight months of talks, the parties had stopped speaking to each other and the NLRB assigned a mediator to bring them together. The union, represented by Robert Ozanne, was aiming for a thirteen-cent-per-hour raise ("in conformity with the national pattern") and a five-day workweek; the store would only offer three cents more per hour and desired to retain the option for a six-day week. The union local put pressure on the store to return to the bargaining table by distributing leaflets to shoppers passing by on the sidewalk. For its part, the store, which utilized the Mountain States Employers Council as its bargaining agent, maintained that the complexity of the wage structure meant that the thirteen- versus three-cent argument was a false comparison and that its offer was fair.

The dispute took a detour in August, as the AF of L's statewide meeting (held in Denver) barred the press from covering their delegates' discussion of whom to endorse in the Democratic primary for the governor's race, incumbent Ed Johnson or the more liberal challenger, Eugene Debs Cervi. The *Denver Post*, under the editorship of E. Palmer Hoyt, chided the union and Ozanne for stifling press freedom, contrary to "one of the primary tenets of liberalism, the right of the people 'to know.'" Ozanne asked for, and received, space for an op-ed rebuttal. He wrote that the union, as a strictly private organization, had every right not to have its closed-door debate covered, just as the chamber of commerce was able to debate its endorsements in private. He further chastised the *Post* for devoting more ink to the union's barring of the press from its deliberations than it had given to its ongoing dispute with "a downtown department store." Implicit

PLEASE DON'T BUY HERE

$30 Per Week IS NOT A LIVING WAGE

Yet a Majority of Denver Dry Employees Receive Less Than This in Take Home Pay.

THE EMPLOYEES HAVE AGREED TO ABIDE BY THE DECISION OF A NEUTRAL PERSON IN ORDER TO ACHIEVE A PEACEABLE SETTLEMENT OF THIS 8-MONTH-OLD WAGE DISPUTE.

MANAGEMENT HAS REFUSED SETTLEMENT BY A NEUTRAL PERSON.

Please Sign a Card at the Door Notifying the Denver Dry Goods Co. That You Will Not Buy Anything Here Until the Company Agrees to Arbitration.

318 Insurance Bldg.
Denver, Colo.

Retail Clerks Union
Local 454, AF of L.

A STORE WHICH REFUSES A PEACEABLE SETTLEMENT DOES NOT DESERVE YOUR PATRONAGE.

Flier handed to people passing by on the sidewalk outside the downtown store in 1948. *Denver Public Library, Western History Collection.*

in his criticism was the idea that perhaps the paper didn't want to alienate one of its largest advertisers by giving the union more coverage than store management might have liked.

The *Post* was, in fact, covering the dispute, if not as lavishly as Ozanne preferred, and its articles gave both sides roughly equal amounts of attention. Two days after Ozanne's op-ed piece, the paper described a new phase of the ongoing "cold strike," with members of the Retail Clerks Union calling for a boycott until the store returned to negotiations and staging picket lines in front of the building. Management finally returned with an offer a few months later, during the all-important holiday shopping season. The local held an election, rejecting the offer and continuing the boycott ("including Santa Claus")[120] and picket line. It wasn't until February 1949 that the store and the local finally reached a settlement, fourteen months after negotiations had begun. Pay for beginning employees was increased to $30.00 per week (up from $27.50), with raises at six months to $32.50 and at one year to $35.

Not all relations between store management and staff were adversarial during the postwar period. As always, management continued to foster harmony and loyalty through ceremonies and events. The main one was the annual dinner of the DDG Five Plus Club, begun in 1945, and held in the Tea Room. All employees with five years or more of service were invited, and since a great many considered their jobs as careers, longevity rates were high. Between five and six hundred people typically attended. Management gave club members handsome lapel pins. These were initially designed with a green background and gold letters, surrounded by a laurel wreath, but were updated in later years as the store's graphic designs changed with columbine blue and finally brown backgrounds. Employees with fifty or more years of service (and there were often several old-timers celebrating golden anniversaries) received fifty silver dollars at the dinner.[121]

In addition to the Five Plus Club, the store sponsored a women's basketball team. In 1949, one player, Phyllis Lockwood, was so talented that she was named to the All-American Women's AAU Squad. The Denver also organized an annual trip to the Central City Opera, in that historic mining town in the foothills west of Denver. The store sponsored and subsidized these summer trips, but they were not free. In 1952, employees were charged $10.98 per couple, which included tickets to the opera (Puccini's *La Bohème* that year), bus transportation and a fried chicken picnic lunch; these outings were so popular that the entire opera house would be filled with several hundred Denver Dry Goods employees and their spouses or dates. Every summer there were also Denver Dry Goods days at Elitch Gardens amusement park at West Thirty-Eighth Avenue and Tennyson Street in northwest Denver.[122]

One longtime employee took a wrong turn. Although head cashier Norman D. Tharp had worked for The Denver for more than fifty years, beginning as a "doorboy" at age nine, store officials discovered in 1954 that he had somehow embezzled $111,000 (the equivalent of about $1.36 million today) from the store's accounts. They were in the middle of an annual audit when Tharp, a widower, was found dead of carbon monoxide poisoning in the garage of his Lakewood home. Although store president Frank Johns had not yet confronted him about the missing money, after Tharp's suicide the store filed a claim against his estate. Two other parties claimed the estate, which his executor valued at about $27,000 (essentially the value of his home and automobile): his widowed sister and a woman named Marcella Volden, who said she was his common-law wife after having lived with him for more than two years. Volden, coincidentally, worked for Daniels and Fisher and was listed as living at an address different from Tharp's, thus giving lie to her

The Denver Dry Goods Women's Basketball Team members pose with their manager; All-Star Phyllis Lockwood stands second from right, circa 1949. *Linda Lebsack collection.*

common-law marriage claim; several months later, she married someone else and moved to San Francisco. Despite a yearlong investigation by the store's attorney, Thomas J. Morrissey, and the Denver district attorney's office, the money was never found, although the DA's office claimed to have found evidence of a "secret playboy life" that led him to spend the missing money on entertainment. The city's newspapers gave the story plenty of coverage, the perfect juicy crime saga involving money, sex and death.[123]

In the 1960s, the store's most famous employee was a very different sort from the accused embezzler of the 1950s. Considered the most glamorous woman in the city, Marilyn VanDerbur joined The Denver in 1965 as a "fashion consultant." The daughter of Denver's Olinger Mortuary president Francis S. VanDerbur, she had been crowned Miss America in 1958 and had spent the years since as television hostess of the annual Miss America Pageant and making commercials for AT&T and the Timex Watch Company. Her role at The Denver was to work closely with Associated Dry Goods' fashion director Maggie De Mille and to preside at fashion shows.[124]

RACE RELATIONS

After the labor tensions of 1947–48, The Denver's management did not face another situation in which it had to rethink its position on a major social justice issue until 1962. By this time, The Denver, still arguably the city's premier department store (facing stronger competition after the 1958 opening of May-D&F described in chapter 7), became the target of civil rights activists who saw its hiring practices as racially discriminatory. The Denver chapter of the Congress of Racial Equality (CORE) charged the store with "illegal and discriminatory hiring practices" because no African Americans (CORE utilized the then-common term "Negro") were employed in the store's offices or on the sales floors, either downtown or in the branches.[125] In July, CORE began picketing the stores, handing out leaflets to shoppers and carrying signs. Not all CORE members were African American; many, perhaps close to half, were white. As with the Montgomery, Alabama 1955–56 bus boycott or the Greensboro, South Carolina 1960 Woolworth lunch counter sit-ins, Denver's CORE members weren't about to allow the leading store in their city escape the spotlight.

Store president Frank Johns responded by pointing out that 5.0 percent of the store's employees were black, though only 3.5 percent of the Denver area's population was African American. Johns told the press that if the store were to accede to CORE's demands (which he termed an "ultimatum"), it would be tantamount to discrimination against its longtime employees, some of whom might have to be let go in order to hire more black employees. This was not the best argument; today, most people would see it as Johns trying too hard to justify his position and being on the wrong side of history. CORE responded to Johns by pointing out that while some African Americans were employed by the store, all of them were in "menial" jobs, with none allowed to interact with customers in a sales or service capacity. With over eight hundred salesclerks, CORE asked why it was that none were African American. The Denver Police Department got involved when it issued littering citations to four female CORE members handing out leaflets, after a complaint by a city engineer named Clarence Hill. CORE vice-president Richard Rapp questioned the citations' legality, arguing that they violated the First Amendment right of free speech, and Denver judge Robert P. Fullerton agreed that the citations were invalid, but only because they quoted the wrong city ordinance, having to do with distribution of leaflets on private property. Sidewalks were public.

The CORE protest lasted several weeks but ended in late August when the civil rights organization and the store reached an agreement (the terms of which remained secret) that called for the hiring of African Americans for sales and office positions. Three African Americans immediately joined the store as new hires, and CORE withdrew its picket lines, calling for more people of color to apply for jobs with the store.

LIFE AT THE TOP

Frank J. Johns, as mentioned in chapter 7, became president of The Denver Dry Goods Company in 1948, after having serving for twelve years in various capacities. Johns hailed from the small farming town of Moline, Kansas, where his father had run a general store and where his grandfather on his mother's side, a Civil War veteran, had homesteaded. Johns was elevated to the presidency when his predecessor, Charles A. Shinn, became chairman of the board. By 1968, it was time for Johns to do the same (Shinn having retired from the board in 1957 after fifty-one years of service to the store). During his tenure, Johns had overseen not only the complete modernization of the downtown store but also The Denver's first forays into satellite locations:

Cherry Creek, Lakeside, Greeley, Boulder, Cinderella City and Northglenn, along with a modern new warehouse in 1953 at 50 South Kalamath Street that included a budget home furnishings store. As Shinn had done before him, he would remain involved with the store for several more years as chairman, as well as chief executive officer. No future president of the store would serve for as many years as he had done.[126]

To succeed Johns as president, The Denver's parent company Associated Dry Goods transferred forty-seven-year-old Walker Douglas Poole, a former World War II fighter pilot, from the Cincinnati division, H. & S. Pogue Company. Poole's career had been very different from that of Johns, who had spent most of his working life at The Denver. Poole had served comparatively brief periods of time at several stores in widely scattered cities—White House in San Francisco, Bon Marche in Seattle and Titche-Goettinger in Dallas—prior to his move to Cincinnati. Under Poole, The Denver opened its branches in Colorado Springs and Southglenn and in

Denver Dry Goods president Frank J. Johns emerges on horseback from the Teller House Bar in Central City, Colorado, in 1954, as part of a Roundup Riders of the Rockies event. Behind his horse stands professional rodeo star Montie Montana Jr. *Denver Public Library, Western History Collection.*

1971 completed a top-to-bottom remodeling of the Cherry Creek branch, by now one of the top performing (in sales per square foot) stores in the entire Associated Dry Goods chain. Under Poole, the downtown store hosted a series of annual themed fortnights, as described in chapter 8, that were meant to bring shoppers back to the flagship. Poole also oversaw the store's new identity program, introduced in 1974: gone was the old columbine blue and white graphic scheme, replaced with a deep-brown signature color and a new, more casual cursive logo in white that looked like someone's actual handwriting (along with changing "The" to "the"). Despite also serving as vice-president of Associated Dry Goods Company, in 1975 Poole resigned from The Denver and its parent to take a job elsewhere.[127]

Succeeding Poole was Carrick A. Hill, who was forty-two years old in 1975 and was coming to The Denver from Associated's Los Angeles operation, J.W. Robinson Company (having previously worked for Macy's in New York and Strawbridge & Clothier in Philadelphia). Yet another in the store's long tradition of Irish or Irish American merchants, Hill, a native of Memphis, Tennessee, was a dynamic figure, launching the Aurora Mall branch and laying plans for expansion to Pueblo and Billings, Montana. He was such a talented executive that he lasted as president for only two years: in 1977, Associated promoted him to a regional executive vice-presidential position, overseeing not only The Denver but also divisions in Indianapolis, Minneapolis and Louisville, Kentucky. He later left Associated, returned to Denver and opened a men's fine clothing store in Cherry Creek North.[128]

To replace Hill, Associated next chose an even younger man, Samuel J. Gerson, thirty-six years old in 1978 when he became president of the store. Hailing from Boston, where he had been general merchandise manager of Filene's department store after receiving his master of business administration from Boston University, Gerson credited "women's lib" as the driving force propelling The Denver and other fashion retailers enjoying success in the 1970s. Yet Gerson, like Hill before him, was destined to be president for only two years before Associated transferred him to its Pittsburgh division, Joseph Horne Company, in early 1979.[129]

The leadership position of The Denver was becoming a revolving door: after Johns had stepped down as president, the store had seen three leaders in a little more than a decade. Each of these men had their own strengths (and weaknesses) and different ideas about how to grow sales. Unfortunately for The Denver, its market share position relative to rivals May-D&F and Joslin's was beginning to slip; it reported a decline in income for fiscal 1978, despite record sales. Executives at Associated sensed it was time for some stability at The Denver, and for the next generation of leadership, it chose to divide responsibilities between a president and a chief executive officer, in what it termed "tandem management." The new men were Thomas L. Roach as chief executive officer and F. Joseph Hayes as president. Roach hailed from Associated's Sunshine State division, Robinson's of Florida, while Hayes, who had been at The Denver since 1975, recently serving as its vice-president and chief financial officer, had previously worked at Associated's Sibley's (Rochester, New York) division and at Garfinkel's (Washington, D.C.). Roach would oversee merchandising and advertising, while Hayes would instill financial discipline. At the time of their appointments, Roach was thirty-six years old, and Hayes was thirty-seven. This would be a young men's game.[130]

The new team inherited a thirteen-store chain that was lacking momentum and losing ground to rivals. Roach, in charge of merchandising and general direction, recognized that Colorado shoppers did not have a clear picture of what The Denver represented. Everyone knew the store, but the various leaders since Johns had each had different ideas about merchandising, fashion and pricing. Décor at many locations was looking dated, and rivals were aggressively gaining market share any way they could, but especially through sharp pricing and sales promotions. Roach and Hayes decided that for The Denver to regain its dominance, they would have to go back to basics. It would become the premier destination for the shopper seeking quality and value. Goods would not always be the cheapest, but customers would know they had paid a fair price—a return to the policies of Sheedy, Owen, Shinn and Johns. Under Roach and Hayes, The Denver regained a measure of its former luster, a classier alternative to May-D&F and Joslin's. During Roach's and Hayes's tenure at the helm, The Denver would become one of Associated Dry Goods' most profitable divisions.[131]

11

THE END COMES

"You're kidding," said Kathryn Jacobs, who was at The Denver in the Cherry Creek Shopping Center [when news broke of the closure]. *"This is a joke, right?"*[132]

WHAT TO DO WITH DOWNTOWN?

One of the new team's primary difficulties was the downtown store. Frank Johns had built the city's first branch department store nearly three decades earlier, and with each new one there were fewer reasons for shoppers to make the trek downtown, find a place to park and traipse through nearly 400,000 square feet of merchandise when they had the choice of staying closer to home, parking for free and perusing a smaller (but still well stocked), easier-to-shop branch. To solve parking, the store worked out a deal with Neusteter's, its rival across the alley. Neusteter's realty division had purchased property adjacent to the store (running southwest to Fifteenth Street), demolished the buildings that had stood there and in 1974 built a seven-level parking garage. Neusteter's soon discovered keeping its garage full wasn't easy, so it approached The Denver. Soon, a pedestrian bridge over the alley connected one of the garage's upper levels to the third floor of The Denver. Customers could park (free with validation) in Neusteter's garage, take its elevator to the appropriate level and enter The Denver's third floor, where they were just a few steps away from an elevator or escalator. This put The Denver on par with May-D&F, which had boasted parking directly below its downtown store since its 1958 opening.[133]

But ample parking could not change the fact that customers still had to drive some distance in heavy traffic to get downtown. The Denver, along with the other Sixteenth Street stores, began to rely more on downtown office workers stopping by on lunch hours than it did on destination shoppers. The fortnights had been an attempt to create positive energy downtown, but once they were over, people didn't then shift their habits. Local malls were simply too convenient.

To create a destination that would be as appealing to shoppers as the suburban centers, downtown boosters began as early as the 1950s to talk about creating a pedestrian mall on Sixteenth Street; these were rapidly gaining currency among planners and businesspeople. Where the funding would come from and who would be in charge of building it were details that remained to be worked out, and several years passed with no concrete plans. In 1973, Downtown Denver Inc. (predecessor to today's Downtown Denver Partnership) tried hard to get a mall built, going so far as to commission a design from the Chicago architectural firm C.F. Murphy Associates. Construction, to be financed through assessments on property owners, was proposed for 1975, but it ran into heated opposition from several Sixteenth Street merchants (particularly Myron Neusteter) and building owners and ultimately died.

Finally, the Regional Transportation District (RTD, which ran and still runs the metropolitan area's public transportation system), seeking a way to solve its primary downtown problem of too many buses clogging streets during rush hours, proposed a "transitway mall" along Sixteenth Street. Free shuttle buses would link bus terminals at either end, allowing their system to function more efficiently. RTD hired I.M. Pei and Partners (architects of Courthouse Square, home to May-D&F) to design it and managed to win funding from the federal Department of Transportation to cover a great portion of the cost. Construction began in 1980 and was completed in 1982. The Denver was a major anchor for what Downtown Denver Inc. hoped would be the mall's primary fringe benefit: attracting shoppers to come downtown again.[134]

For its part, The Denver was not one of the Sixteenth Street Mall's naysayers. CEO Tom Roach looked forward to its completion, telling a *Rocky Mountain News* reporter that "the mall will definitely be good for our business; we're right in the center." He wasn't worried either about the project's two-year construction period, certain that customers would "accept this as a

The Regional Transportation District commissioned this architectural model of their Sixteenth Street "Transitway" Mall, featuring the all-important Denver Dry Goods and Neusteter's block, to show citizens what the mall would look like, circa 1979. *Denver Public Library, Western History Collection.*

minor problem."[135] He and store president F. Joseph Hayes got funding from Associated for significant remodeling and improvement projects, signaling their confidence. But they didn't believe that the downtown store needed as much space as it had and ultimately found a way to repurpose the Sixteenth Street side of the basement, leasing it in 1981 to Denver-based sporting goods retailer Gart Brothers. This old Denver firm carried very few products that directly competed with The Denver's offerings, and its leasing the basement generated additional income to keep the department store viable. Eliminating the bargain basement departments (simultaneously shedding bargain departments in suburban stores) also dovetailed with Roach's efforts to bring The Denver's fashion merchandising up several notches.

After the mall was built, The Denver was spruced up with chic new awnings, circa 1985. *Denver Public Library, Western History Collection.*

A section of the women's fragrance and cosmetics department in the downtown store, seen during the store's final decade. *Jim O'Hagan collection.*

Roach remained at the helm of The Denver for six years, until Associated decided to promote him in March 1986 to the position of chairman and chief executive officer of a much larger division, J.W. Robinson of Los Angeles. Having restored The Denver to greater profitability, he had "accomplished all [he] had set out to do," and the parent company needed him to do the same in Southern California. Store president F. Joseph Hayes would remain in Denver, and in June 1986, Associated moved another career executive to Denver to replace Roach, a forty-nine-year-old named Stanley Zweck-Bronner who had previously been with Ivey's of Florida. The final chief executive officer of The Denver would enjoy his new position for less than one year.[136]

GOODBYE TO ALL THAT

Only sixteen days after the announcement that Zweck-Bronner would be The Denver's new CEO came much bigger news: Associated had been in merger talks with May Department Stores Company for nearly two years, and May had made an offer. With a total value of $2.7 billion, May proposed giving Associated's owners $66 in May stock per outstanding share of Associated stock. After Associated rejected this offer as too low on June 24 (four days after it was made), May board chairman David C. Farrell "turned up the heat," coming back with a *lower* offer of $60 per share (but in cash rather than stock, making it sweeter for investors) that he hoped would force Associated back into negotiations. The Associated board saw this as a hostile takeover attempt and enacted a shareholder rights plan (often called a "poison pill defense") that stipulated that if May, or any other entity, were to obtain 50 percent or more of its stock, Associated would have the right to issue new shares, increasing the total number outstanding tremendously, from 35 million to up to 120 million new shares, making a takeover nearly impossible. Farrell, who had been May's chief executive officer since 1979, was hoping to grow what was already the nation's third-largest department store chain into a much bigger entity that could better compete with the largest, Federated Department Stores. Federated in 1985 had posted sales of $9.98 billion; adding Associated's $4.4 billion in sales to May's $5 billion would make May a close number two.[137]

On July 16, all speculation ended. The two boards came together to announce a modified version of the first deal, essentially a friendly takeover. Associated shareholders would receive 0.86 shares of May stock for each Associated stock they owned, valuing the transaction at $2.53 billion, or $61.81 per share based on that day's prices. Thoughts about what would happen in Colorado, which had been in the air since the news broke of the first offer, began to focus on the notion that both The Denver and May-D&F would continue to operate as before. Retail analysts thought it likely that May-D&F would continue to serve the "broad middle," while The Denver, which had begun a more upscale trajectory under Roach, would be positioned even higher, in order to compete with luxury retailers expected to enter the Colorado market when the new enclosed mall at Cherry Creek opened, projected for 1988. (Replacing a significant portion of Temple Buell's original center, it would open in 1990.) The Denver was already on board to be an anchor, as was Saks Fifth Avenue; upscaling The Denver would allow May to compete more effectively with Saks and any other anchor (such as Neiman Marcus, long rumored to be interested in Denver) that might enter the

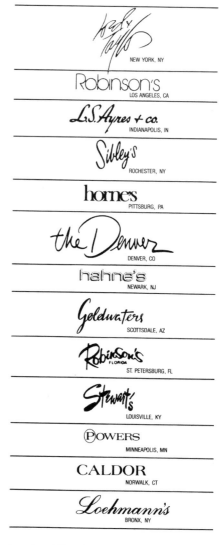

Associated Dry Goods Company boasted an impressive roster of names, as seen in this page from a circa 1983 Denver Dry Goods recruitment brochure. *Jim O'Hagan collection.*

market. As for the two Sixteenth Street stores, with a combined size of about 750,000 square feet, downtown boosters were sanguine. "It certainly wouldn't be bad, and it could be a plus," Downtown Denver Inc. president Richard C.D. Fleming told reporters, basing his optimism on the idea that

The Denver would be repositioned as a more exclusive store. He said he doubted that either of the two flagship stores would close.[138]

Another reason why observers thought that not much would change after the merger was that May, as had been avowed many times over the years by its executives and spokesmen, always aimed to be the dominant operator of department stores in all of its markets. In Denver, while The Denver and May-D&F had been duking it out for decades for the middle- and upper-middle-income shopper, mutual rival Joslin's had quietly assumed the top slot. Joslin's had sales in Colorado of approximately $205 million, to May-D&F's $172 million and The Denver's $145 million; combining May-D&F and The Denver would create a $300 million–plus behemoth. If May were to entirely close down Associated's Colorado division, May-D&F would still be in second place behind Joslin's. Some worried that the federal government might view the merger negatively, worried about antitrust concerns not only in Colorado but also in Southern California and Pennsylvania, where the two companies had long battled. As events would soon show, it wouldn't be the Federal Trade Commission that worried about competition but officials closer to home.[139]

In late January 1987, The Denver's president, F. Joseph Hayes, was on vacation with his family when he received a phone call from his new May Department Stores Company boss in St. Louis. Leaving his wife and children to enjoy their vacation, Hayes flew home. On Friday, January 30, he placed 5:30 a.m. telephone calls to managers of all of The Denver's stores, instructing them to report downtown by 7:00 a.m. When they assembled, he announced the sad news, although most probably had expected what was coming: after nearly ninety-two years, The Denver Dry Goods Company was no more. He had called them to the store so early because at 10:00 a.m. May headquarters would be issuing a press release, and he didn't want them to hear about the closure through the news media (which is how he had heard of the original buyout offer the previous summer), and needed them to be prepared for the onslaught of questions they'd receive from their employees and customers. Not all locations would actually close: some would be converted to branches of May-D&F. But The Denver, as an entity, would disappear.[140]

Reaction was swift and tearful, as recounted in this book's introduction. People could just not believe that such a permanent-seeming institution could just disappear through corporate machinations. Weren't The Denver's stores just as busy and beautiful as they had always been, despite the weak Colorado economy? How could executives one thousand miles away just decide to abolish a major local institution? But if the first stage of grief is denial, the second one is anger.

Within two weeks, Colorado governor Roy Romer, along with the state's attorney general Duane Woodard and Denver mayor Federico Peña, called for an investigation. The politicians were deeply disappointed with May for not trying to sell The Denver whole to another retailer. Romer had had conversations with Alex Dillard, executive vice-president of the Little Rock, Arkansas–based Dillard's chain. Dillard told him he had inquired about buying The Denver outright, as a full package, but May executives had said they already had commitments for some locations. Romer had also phoned May officials in St. Louis, who told him the same thing, that they already had buyers for some stores and weren't interested in a Dillard's offer. Romer felt the main reason May would not want to sell The Denver whole was to reduce competition, which would result in fewer choices and higher prices for Colorado consumers. The three men gave a press conference,

The Denver's local executives continued to commit to the health of the downtown flagship right up to the end, including this remodeled first-floor men's department. Workers completed the project after the announcement of the store's closure, just before the going-out-of-business sale. *Jim O'Hagan collection.*

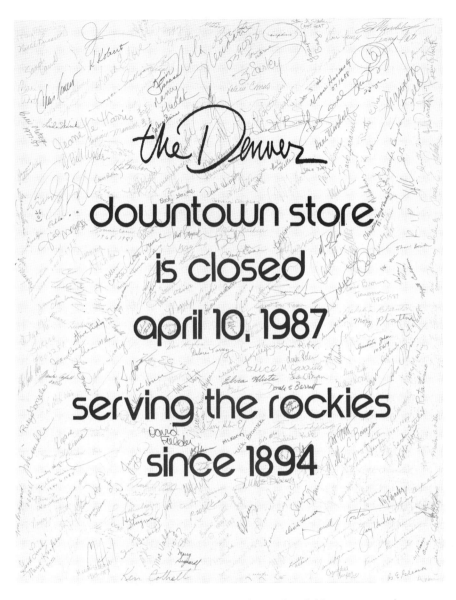

On the very last day of operation, downtown employees signed this commemorative poster, many including their employee numbers or dates of service. *Jim O'Hagan collection.*

promising to "play legal hardball" with May unless it replaced The Denver with truly competitive stores: not middle-of-the-road chains like J.C. Penney, for example, but with stores at the same level as The Denver, Dillard's or something like them. Broadway Southwest, a division of Carter-Hawley-

Hale Stores, was another possibility; it had recently opened three department stores in area malls. Joslin's also might make a good replacement at some malls where it didn't already operate. Woodard threatened an antitrust lawsuit if May were to sell the stores to a "lower-tier" operator. Romer and Peña were also concerned about the fate of the vast downtown store; Romer suggested May donate it to the city or the Downtown Denver Partnership "as a goodwill gesture."[141]

Despite the governor's efforts to keep competition robust and jobs from disappearing, his recent electoral opponent for the governorship, state senator Ted Strickland, was sharply critical. Strickland opined that it was "absolutely the wrong message to send to corporate America," potentially scaring other retailers from coming to the state. Bill Schultz, president of the Colorado Retail Council, concurred, questioning why the governor chose to "fight this thing on the front page of newspapers," especially since May had always been "an excellent corporate citizen." But Richard C.D. Fleming of the Downtown Denver Partnership was supportive of Romer's strategy of making the fight public, particularly after early efforts to work behind the scenes had borne no fruit. "When the governor of Colorado calls the president of the May Company in St. Louis, and he's told that the president of the May is in his office but can't talk to the governor, that's not cooperating," Fleming said. Romer countered the criticism himself, comparing the situation to what would happen "if United Airlines offered to buy Continental Airlines" (both had hubs in Denver at the time): it would be a major public policy issue.[142]

The fight soon lost steam. In early March, May announced the deals it had made for the stores that it did not want to convert to May-D&F, and the politicians took no further action, recognizing that the game was up.[143] The disposition of The Denver Dry Goods Company would be as follows:

- Downtown would close no later than May 1, 1987. The building's afterlife is told in the epilogue.
- Cherry Creek would become May-D&F and move to the new mall. Fellow former Associated division Lord & Taylor would join it. The 1953 Denver Dry Goods building still stands as of this writing.
- Lakeside would close, with the liquidation sale beginning immediately. The mall was later demolished.
- Northglenn would become May-D&F. The mall closed in 1994 and was demolished.

- Cinderella City would become May-D&F. The mall eventually closed and was mostly demolished.
- Colorado Springs Citadel would be sold to Mervyn's, a discount chain (now defunct). The mall remains open as of this writing.
- Boulder Crossroads would close. The mall eventually closed and was mostly demolished.
- Fort Collins would be sold to Mervyn's. The Denver's former building was later demolished.
- Southglenn would be sold to J.C. Penney. The Denver's building was later demolished, along with most of the mall.
- Aurora Mall would be converted to the women's departments of May-D&F, with the original May-D&F building retained for men's and home departments. Later, May consolidated into The Denver's former building. It remains open as Macy's as of this writing.
- Pueblo would be sold to Mervyn's. The mall still stands as of this writing.
- Billings still stands; Dillard's now occupies The Denver's spot (Billings had closed prior to the May merger).
- Southwest Plaza would be sold to J.C. Penney, which continues to operate it as of this writing.

Greeley had been closed earlier in the 1980s, as part of Tom Roach's and F. Joseph Hayes's efforts to turn The Denver into the most profitable division of Associated Dry Goods; it was later demolished.

Once May-D&F, Mervyn's and J.C. Penney made their announcements, May began liquidation sales downtown and at the locations those retailers would be acquiring. Downtown closed on Thursday, April 10, just a month or so shy of what would have been the ninety-third anniversary of Dennis Sheedy's founding of the institution. The final closures of the stores that would be sold followed on April 30. The Denver Dry Goods Company was lost to history.[144]

AFTERMATH

How dismayed Dennis Sheedy, William R. Owen and Charles A. Shinn would have been at the closure of what had been so central to their lives. For his part, Frank J. Johns, who was still alive, blamed Associated for running a good store into the ground by putting too much faith in people with master of business administration (MBA) degrees. In reality, it had nothing to do with how store executives had been educated; rather, it was part of a wave of department store consolidations that had begun many years earlier and would continue for many years into the future.

Duane Woodard would have his day in court with May Department Stores Company after all, but it was not for violation of antitrust laws. Instead, it would be for May-D&F's propensity to run nearly permanent sales, attempting to create what he charged was a false sense of getting a bargain when in fact the "original price" on a price tag was essentially a fiction. He sued the company in 1989 and won in court the following year. But May Department Stores Company would not be around forever. It would continue making acquisitions throughout the 1990s and into the 2000s, including Chicago's Marshall Field & Company, arguably the greatest of all American department stores. In 1993, May decided to cut costs by consolidating several divisions. In Colorado, this meant that May-D&F stores would no longer bear that local name and would instead become Foley's, an extension of a Houston-based chain it had recently acquired. Foley's signage went up on May-D&F (and some former Denver Dry Goods) buildings, but would only remain there for a dozen years. In 2005, May reached an agreement with Cincinnati-based Federated Department Stores to be acquired in a deal that would create the nation's largest department store chain, with nearly one thousand locations (at that time). Federated had purchased Macy's in 1994 and after the merger would rename all of the acquired stores as Macy's (a select few as Bloomingdale's, which it also owned) and change its own name to Macy's Inc. As of this writing, Macy's Inc. still exists but has been steadily closing stores for several years and investing significant sums in its online retail operations.[145]

Epilogue

A LANDMARK'S
NEW BEGINNING

*In a city built with brick and stone, much of it replaced by concrete and glass,
it's like a long-lost relative showing up at a reunion. No one recognizes him, but
everyone is glad he's back.*[146]

THE WHITE ELEPHANT

When the downtown Denver Dry Goods store closed, there was much
consternation among city boosters.[147] The Sixteenth Street Mall was not
quite five years old, and its largest store was gone. In February, as recounted
previously, Governor Roy Romer had suggested that May Department
Stores Company consider donating it to the city or the Downtown Denver
Partnership. May regularly made philanthropic donations, but giving away a
half block in a major city's downtown was more than it was prepared to do.
It hired an appraiser, who determined a value of approximately $16 million.
It would take several years and many false starts, but eventually, the white
elephant of Sixteenth Street (literally, Frank E. Edbrooke's original red brick
and limestone buildings had been obscured by cream or white paint since
1936) would emerge as a renovated jewel in the heart of Denver.

Even before the closure, a potential white knight emerged: Jim Sullivan,
president of Sullivan, Hayes and Company. In February 1987, he announced
a $26 million plan to convert the building into a vertical mall, with shops,
restaurants and a six-screen movie theater. He was a retail man; he ruled
out office or residential components because he had never developed such

uses. He envisioned atriums with dramatic fountains and glass elevators and a reopened Tea Room; an unnamed "well-known" out-of-state retailer would occupy three levels of the Fifteenth Street building as anchor. Sullivan pointed to the success of the Shops at Tabor Center, a 1984 multilevel enclosed mall several blocks down Sixteenth Street, and said his "Denver Galleria" would be just as popular.

Costs soon grew to $40 million, and Sullivan struggled to sign his anchor. In November, he said, "We have something to prove to them [the unnamed retailer] about downtown." Another Denver developer, Cambridge Development Group, headed by Allen Gerstenberger and Jeff Selby, saw opportunity in Sullivan's troubles and announced its own plan. Cambridge, which had earlier renovated other downtown buildings, was finishing up its conversion of the former Neusteter's store into apartments. Gerstenberger met with the Denver Urban Renewal Authority (DURA), a city agency soliciting proposals on a fifteen-block area of downtown it deemed blighted. DURA had earlier made its mark downtown with its Skyline Urban Renewal Project, a twenty-seven-block area below Curtis Street; it purchased most of the buildings in Skyline, demolished them and

The paint stripped away, The Denver Dry Goods Building, one of the largest renovation projects in Denver history, as seen just before the 1993 opening of Media Play. *Denver Public Library, Western History Collection, photograph by Roger Whitacre.*

sold the land to developers. But that had occurred in the 1960s and 1970s; by the late 1980s, DURA, particularly after Susan Powers had become its director, was taking a more preservation-friendly approach to urban renewal.

Suddenly, a third suitor appeared. Another Denver entity, Jamis Corporation, announced it had signed a deal with May to buy the building; funds would be coming from a "very wealthy group of third-, fourth-, and fifth-generation Denverites." May's price for the property continued to be the appraised $16 million, and Jamis promised to raise it. Its plan was similar to Cambridge's, mostly residential with a retail component; Jamis also hoped to revive the Tea Room. Similar to Sullivan's plan, Jamis wanted an anchor for a significant portion of the Fifteenth Street building.

Stakes for redevelopment ratcheted higher in late 1987, when Denver City Council voted to build a new convention center on a large tract bounded by Fourteenth, Welton and Stout Streets and Speer Boulevard. Suddenly, the white elephant was hot property: California Street would be the primary pedestrian corridor between the convention center and the Sixteenth Street Mall. Sullivan was not giving up, despite Cambridge's and Jamis's announcements, but said he was unwilling to pay May's price, given renovation difficulties he anticipated and Denver's depressed real estate market; he would pay $12 million but no more.

In March 1988, DURA changed the game. Concerned the various suitors were going nowhere, with an important site in danger of remaining vacant for some time, it announced an agreement with May to buy the property for only $6 million, a significant discount. Under this deal, May would claim the remaining $10 million on its taxes as a charitable deduction. Perhaps Governor Romer's earlier notion that May consider the building as a potential tax shelter had influenced its executives, but more likely, May was a department store operator, not a real estate company—it wanted to be free of this albatross. DURA announced it would award Cambridge development rights, but first Cambridge had to prove its financial ability; some of its earlier projects were in default. DURA told Cambridge to come up with an equity partner. City council voted $3.5 million from the city's Housing Trust Council to assist DURA in the purchase; the renewal agency would have to come up with the balance through other means. Ultimately, these other funding sources included the AFL-CIO's Colorado Building Trades Council, First Interstate Bank, Women's Bank and Dominion Bank.

May and DURA finalized the sale in July 1988. Development seemed immanent, but Cambridge struggled. In December, Cambridge announced a partnership with United Artists Cinemas, which would open a multiplex in the building and help fund other parts of the project; Deerpath, a Chicago firm, would also invest. DURA imposed a July 1989 deadline for Cambridge to complete its financial package, but Deerpath pulled out, forcing Cambridge to withdraw. Although Denver had struggled through the second half of the 1980s, by 1989 its economy was beginning to strengthen. So when Powers asked for new proposals by mid-September, five different entities submitted ideas. Three were local, while two hailed from elsewhere.

Of the local firms bidding, the most intriguing proposal came from David French and Wally B. Hultin. French had earlier used an innovative financial structure (office condominiums) for his renovation of the Daniels and Fisher Tower, the landmark built by The Denver's one-time rival, shorn of its supporting department store building in 1971. French put together that project after four previous attempts to rescue the tower had failed. For the Denver Dry Goods Building, he and Hultin proposed a "European style" 120-room hotel, a reopened Tea Room and a cinema. French's friend Dana Crawford, known for her earlier Larimer Square (which included the Granite Building, one-time home of McNamara Dry Goods) and Oxford Hotel projects, was another bidder; her plan called for residential, office and retail uses, along with a daycare center, reopened Tea Room and bakery. The third local bidder was none other than Cambridge Development Group. Selby and Gerstenberger had already invested much time and money and clearly loved Denver's old buildings. They found a new financial partner, and their plan was similar to Crawford's, adding a community center but making no mention of reopening the Tea Room.

A partnership of Sheraton Hotels, Tishman West and Denver developer Water Street Development came up with the most ambitious plan, a large "headquarters hotel" on the block across Fifteenth Street from The Denver, linked to the store building by a bridge across Fifteenth. The Denver Dry Goods Building would house luxury suites as part of the hotel, along with retail space and a reopened Tea Room. The final proposal (apartments, cinema, retail, reopened Tea Room) came from a consortium of three men: David Walentas of New York; John Benton of Tempe, Arizona; and Charles Kireker of Middleburg, Virginia.

Powers and DURA mulled over their options for a week and on September 29 announced their winner: Walentas/Benton/Kireker (WBK). Powers felt WBK's financial position was stronger than those of the local teams, and WBK was the only bidder prepared to purchase the building from DURA by the end of the year. They didn't close by December 31, however, and in July 1990, Walentas, with his considerable financial resources, pulled out, leaving Benton and Kireker without enough money to proceed. DURA was in a bind; Cambridge had recently declared bankruptcy and was in no position to take on the enormous renovation. Powers didn't want to just put the building up for sale because it then might be demolished, and she was "absolutely committed that it not become another Central Bank situation" (a landmark building that was facing the wrecking ball despite efforts to save it).

THE DENVER DRY GOODS BUILDING REBORN

All was not lost for the Denver Dry Goods Building, however. Sensing an opportunity in Walentas's exit, French and Hultin approached Benton and Kireker, and the four put together a new proposal. Hultin called it the "next great downtown project" but was concerned about scope, wanting to "make it a smaller project" that would be easier to manage. Three months later, Hultin's idea to reduce the scope was given a boost when Robert Waxman Inc. announced it would be entering the project as an anchor, purchasing the Fifteenth Street building. On the ground floor, Waxman would relocate its longtime camera store and open a "Sony-only" electronics shop. On the Sixteenth Street side, the developers were assembling a group of sporting goods retailers to create a recreation-themed mini-mall that would include an indoor climbing wall.

Time passed. The French-led team strived to get started, but per French, the Gulf War and "an uncertain national economy" were making it difficult to land retailers. The housing portion posed its own problems, and in 1991, DURA decided to award development rights for it to New York–based Affordable Housing Development Corporation, headed by Jonathan Rose (the firm has since been renamed Jonathan Rose Companies). Rose was an interesting combination of businessman and idealist. In the 1920s, his father and great uncle had founded Rose Associates, a major New York City residential developer, but Jonathan was more interested in affordable housing than the more upscale projects his family members favored and had struck out on his own. He told the *New York Times* "the 'trickle-down' economic policies of the Reagan and Bush Administrations never trickled enough to serve the housing needs of millions of Americans."[148] For this DURA project, he would create fifty-one one- and two-bedroom apartments in floors three through six

Workmen on scaffolding remove an estimated thirty layers of paint in 1993. *Denver Public Library, Western History Collection, photograph by Steve Groer.*

of the Fifteenth Street building; of these, forty would be "affordable," meaning income-qualified, while the remaining eleven would be leased at prevailing market rates.

In May 1992, DURA decided to shift gears yet again, dismissing the French-led team and giving Rose control of the entire project. This embittered French, who later told an interviewer "we were blindsided...we had a plan ready to go and it was handed to Jonathan on a silver platter." Rose was able to capitalize on Denver's economic upswing and plow ahead. The remaining components soon fell into place. In addition to Robert Waxman Camera and the fifty-one apartments in the Fifteenth Street building, DURA itself would occupy the second floor, with the Denver Metro Convention and Visitors Bureau on three. Plans for the Sixteenth Street building were not fully complete, but discount retailer T.J. Maxx would occupy the second floor, accessed via a new escalator and elevator inside the Sixteenth Street entrance. For suburban-oriented T.J. Maxx, this would be only its second downtown location. Completing the retail development, in July 1993 Musicland Group leased the basement and first floor of the Sixteenth Street building for its then-new chain Media Play, a superstore with music, books, movies and video games.

In March 1993, scaffolding went up. Contractors removed sixty years of paint, an estimated thirty layers, in a months-long process, exposing the building's red brick walls and limestone and sandstone trim for the first time since the Great Depression. Cornices were repainted in rich blue and buff tones. Over the spring and summer, Denverites watched the transformation in amazement: a stunning "new" Victorian building had suddenly appeared in the heart of downtown. Instead of looking like a "big basement freezer," the Denver Dry Goods Building was now an energetic composition, over which "the eye moves, sweeping down a building that looks like it means business," wrote *Rocky Mountain News* art and architecture critic Mary Voelz Chandler.[149]

In October, Robert Waxman and T.J. Maxx both opened their doors to booming business, and apartments quickly filled up with residents excited to be living downtown. Media Play followed in May 1994, giving office workers new reasons to spend money during lunch hours and providing downtown boosters and proud Denverites hosting out-of-town relatives a talking point:

Enjoying his new apartment in the Fifteenth Street building in 1993, Ryan Lyden gazes across parking lots toward May-D&F. *Denver Public Library, Western History Collection; photograph by Dean Krakel.*

In the renovated Fifteenth Street building, Jennifer Takaki (left) and her cousin Alison Takaki (right) contemplate the space. *Denver Public Library, Western History Collection; photograph by Glenn Asakawa.*

Residents of and visitors to the fifth-floor condominiums built in the former Tea Room enjoy this historic photograph collage upon emerging from the elevators. *Photograph by author.*

"Look at what we did with this old department store!" Lost, however, was the original plan to reopen the Tea Room. "Everyone wants to see the Tea Room back, but you just don't have 17,000 square foot restaurants like that anymore," Powers said.[150]

The final component, the for-sale loft condominiums on the third, fourth, fifth and sixth floors, took longer to develop. DURA awarded this phase to a Canadian developer, BCORP of Vancouver, British Columbia, which began construction on sixty-six lofts in late 1997. The Tea Room was subdivided. Fifth-floor residents on Sixteenth- and California Street–facing sides enjoyed access to the restaurant's former promenade (divided into private terraces), while all fifth-floor residents could admire the graceful arches that supported the former Tea Room's ceiling. BCORP installed skylights above the former executive offices for sixth-floor buyers, and those with fourth-floor units enjoyed bi-level living incorporating the mezzanine floor. The loft condominiums were complete by summer 1999. It had taken a dozen years since the store closed to fully renovate and reactivate the old queen of Sixteenth Street, and Denverites and visitors still enjoy its stately presence today.

NOTES

Introduction

1. Jack Kisling, "No More Denver in Denver," *Denver Post*, February 1, 1987.

Chapter 1

2. *Rocky Mountain News*, January 1, 1881.
3. Ibid.; *Denver Post*, April 15, 1953.
4. Hall, *History of the State of Colorado*, 4:509; Vickers, *History of the City of Denver*, 534.
5. Leonard, and Noel, *Denver*, 36–37; census figures per Wikipedia.com, "Denver, CO," accessed May 8, 2016.
6. Bird, *Lady's Life in the Rocky Mountains*, 127–28.
7. Doner, "Denver's Merchant Princes," 27.
8. Noel, *Denver's Larimer Street*, 93.
9. "Denver Dry Goods Company and How It Grew."
10. *Rocky Mountain News*, September 15, 1878; July 6, 1879; August 17, 1879; January 1, 1880.
11. Ibid., March 17, 1880; April 2, 1880; July 4, 1880; January 1, 1881; Doner, "Denver's Merchant Princes," 27, 28. Cassimere is a type of "twill-weave, worsted suiting fabric, often with a striped pattern" (http://dictionary.reference.com/browse/cassimere).
12. Barth, *City People*, 110–47.

13. Noel, *Denver Landmarks*, 11–12; *Denver Republican*, July 3, 1883.

14. Quotations from *Denver Republican*, July 3, 1883; Doner, "Denver's Merchant Princes," 29.

Chapter 2

15. Hall, *History of the State of Colorado*, 4:510.

16. *Rocky Mountain News*, January 1, 1885; October 10, 1885; December 19, 1885; May 5, 1888.

17. *Denver Post*, April 15, 1953.

18. Noel, *Denver Landmarks*, 26–27; *Ballenger & Richards' Seventeenth Annual Denver City Directory*, 56.

19. *Rocky Mountain News*, October 30, 1889.

20. *Denver Republican*, January 3, 1892.

21. Leonard and Noel, *Denver*, 103–5; *Colorado Sun*, July 16, 1893.

22. *Colorado Sun*, September 7, 1893; Noel, *Growing Through History*, 44.

23. Sheedy, *Autobiography of Dennis Sheedy*, 55–56.

24. *Colorado Sun*, September 10, 1893; September 11, 1893.

25. *Denver Times*, May 22, 1894.

26. Hall, *History of Colorado*, 3:180–84; Noel, *Growing Through History*, 1, 41–42.

27. Sheedy, *Autobiography of Dennis Sheedy*, 48.

28. *Denver Post*, November 5, 1904. Prior to his Gaylord Street address, McNamara had previously resided at 2230 East Fourteenth Avenue and, earlier, at Eleventh and Curtis Streets in the Auraria neighborhood.

Chapter 3

29. Unnamed prominent citizen of Denver, quoted in Byers, *Encyclopedia of Biography of Colorado*, 1:221.

30. Unless otherwise noted, this chapter is based on Hall, *History of the State of Colorado*, 4:563–64; Byers, *Encyclopedia of Biography of Colorado*, 1:218–21; Sheedy, *Autobiography of Dennis Sheedy*; Raymond A. Eaton, "Sheedy Made Fortune Thru Own Efforts," *Denver Times*, October 16, 1923.

31. Sheedy, *Autobiography of Dennis Sheedy*, 7; Hall, *History of Colorado*, 4:563.

32. Hall, *History of Colorado*, 4:563.

33. Alvin Daniels was no relation to William Bradley Daniels, founder of Daniels and Fisher; J. Sidney Brown was no relation to Henry Cordes

Brown, later builder of the Brown Palace Hotel, or to J.J. "Johnny" Brown, husband to Margaret Tobin "Molly" Brown of *Titanic* fame. Daniels and Brown were simply very common names in Denver's early history.

34. Sheedy, *Autobiography of Dennis Sheedy*, 18.

35. Ibid., 21.

36. Ibid., 44.

37. He may also have inherited some or all of his shares from Alvin B. Daniels, per Noel, *Growing Through History*, 43.

38. *Denver Times*, October 1, 1898; Noel, *Growing Through History*, 45–46; Noel, *City and the Saloon*, 63.

39. Sheedy, *Autobiography of Dennis Sheedy*, 57.

40. Doner, "Denver's Merchant Princes," 56–57.

41. *Denver Catholic Register*, October 22, 1953, 1–3; *Denver Times*, April 22, 1899; December 8, 1901.

42. Sheedy, *Autobiography of Dennis Sheedy*, 59.

43. Kohl, *Denver's Historic Mansions*, 60.

44. Ibid., 58–62; Noel, *Denver Landmarks*, 41–42; Zimmer, *Denver's Capitol Hill Neighborhood*, 36.

Chapter 4

45. *Rocky Mountain Herald*, November 7, 1896.

46. Sheedy, *Autobiography of Dennis Sheedy*, 56.

47. Byers, *Encyclopedia of Biography of Colorado*, 1:381–82; *Rocky Mountain News*, August 16, 1918.

48. *Denver Republican*, January 1, 1899; Minutes of Denver Dry Goods Company Stockholders' Meeting, May 26, 1896, quoted in Doner, "Denver's Merchant Princes," 46–47; www.measuringworth.com, accessed March 19, 2016.

49. *Rocky Mountain Herald*, November 7, 1896.

50. *Denver Times*, October 3, 1898.

51. Ibid.

52. *Rocky Mountain News*, May 5, 1903; *Denver Times*, January 28, 1902; September 5, 1902; October 24, 1902.

53. *Denver Catholic Register*, December 1, 1919; *Rocky Mountain News*, June 2, 1923; *Denver Republican*, January 1, 1907; *Denver Times*, August 2, 1902; "The Denver Dry Goods Company and How It Grew"; www.measuringworth. com, accessed March 19, 2016.

54. For further information on the rival stores, see the author's *Denver's Sixteenth Street* (Charleston, SC: Arcadia Publishing, 2015), *Lost Denver* (Charleston, SC: Arcadia Publishing, 2015) and *Daniels and Fisher*.
55. *Denver Post*, April 15, 1953; *Denver Times*, March 4, 1899. O'Meara Ford is still in business as of this writing.
56. *Denver Post*, April 15, 1953.
57. Ibid.; May Company advertisement, ibid., December 2, 1906.
58. *Denver Times*, July 26, 1902.
59. Ibid.
60. Ibid.; "Store Manual," undated with 1941 written by hand inside front cover, 89.
61. *Rocky Mountain News*, June 2, 1923.
62. The Denver Dry Goods Company, "Report of Operations for Month of December 1923," 8; measuringworth.com, accessed March 26, 2016. All current values are based on the website's "contemporary standard of living" valuation.

Chapter 5

63. "New Owners of Denver Store to Rapidly Expand Business," *Rocky Mountain News*, February 15, 1924.
64. Ibid., October 16, 1923; December 26, 1958; *Denver Times*, October 26, 1923; www.measuringworth.com, accessed March 26, 2016 ($416,000,000 represents Measuring Worth's "economic power value" valuation).
65. *Rocky Mountain News*, February 15, 1924; *Denver Post*, February 14, 1924; *Denver Times*, October 27, 1923; Minutes of Denver Dry Goods Board Meeting, December 27, 1923, quoted in Doner, "Denver's Merchant Princes," 76–76.
66. Hendrickson, *Grand Emporiums*, 397; *Rocky Mountain News*, April 30, 1948.
67. *Rocky Mountain News*, February 15, 1924. Sadly, Wilkinson did not live long after he became president of The Denver, dying in March 1925 as the result of a toboggan accident. Mayfield replaced him as president, per Doner, "Denver's Merchant Princes," 76.
68. These paragraphs describing the store's departments are based on a house telephone directory from the period immediately after World War II; the basic layout of the departments had been set during the mid-1920s reconfiguration that followed the 1924 addition to the Sixteenth Street building.

Chapter 6

69. Denver Dry Goods advertisement, *Denver Post*, November 29, 1924.

70. "Denver Directions" employee newsletter, June 1977, 4.

71. *Denver Catholic Register*, December 11, 1919, Christmas Supplement.

72. *Denver Post*, November 28, 1924; *Rocky Mountain News*, November 29, 1924.

73. *Denver Post*, April 15, 1953.

74. Ibid.; July 26, 1962; May 15, 1977; "Denver Directions" employee newsletter, November/December 1984, 10–11; James O'Hagan, interview with the author, April 2, 2016. The Herndon Davis portraits are now in the collection of History Colorado, having been donated by store executive James O'Hagan after the store closed. Several have been published in Leavitt and Noel, *Herndon Davis*.

75. *Rocky Mountain News*, May 7, 1971; *Denver Post*, January 31, 1987. Dorothy Howard Kenny was a family friend during the author's childhood.

76. *Rocky Mountain News*, April 19, 1987; *Denver Post*, "Contemporary," February 6, 1977.

77. Author's personal recollection, circa 1970.

78. *Rocky Mountain News*, May 7, 1971.

79. Ibid., February 3, 1987; *Denver Post*, March 4, 1987. These recipes, provided by the tearoom to the newspapers, are reproduced exactly as published.

Chapter 7

80. Frank J. Johns and a framed motto in the store's executive offices, *Denver Post*, May 16, 1965.

81. Longstreth, *American Department Store Transformed 1920–1960*, 34–36.

82. *Denver Post*, January 9, 1931; November 30, 1944; December 9, 1944; July 27, 1948.

83. Ibid., November 9, 1947.

84. Ibid., September 26, 1950; October 1, 1950; October 7, 1950.

85. Ibid., June 24, 1955; May 25, 1958; September 18, 1960; November 22, 1962.

86. Ibid., May 16, 1965.

87. Ibid.; April 13, 1966; August 30, 1966.

88. Ibid., August 14, 1946; May 24, 1967.

89. Zeckendorf, *Autobiography of William Zeckendorf*, 125; *Cervi's*, October 10, 1957; *Rocky Mountain News*, January 17, 1947. For more on the merger of May with Daniels and Fisher, see chapters 5 and 7 of the author's *Daniels and Fisher*.

90. *Denver Post*, April 21, 1964; December 14, 1964; Doner, "Denver's Merchant Princes," 83–84 (Johns's decision to approach Seiler is per an interview she conducted with him on April 4, 1984).

Chapter 8

91. *Rocky Mountain News*, November 14, 1937.

92. This section on the Stockmen's Store is based on multiple sources, including *Cervi's*, July 27, 1950; *Rocky Mountain News*, June 22, 1923; November 14, 1937; November 20, 1945; *Denver Post*, July 17, 1947; "Report of Operations for Month of December 1923" and "The Denver Dry Goods Co. Downtown Store Directory," March 1957.

93. "Gone by the 1970s" per author's conversation with F. Joseph Hayes, February 20, 2016. Hayes joined the store in 1974.

94. *Rocky Mountain News*, September 10, 1964; measuringworth.com, accessed April 17, 2016.

95. *Rocky Mountain News*, April 15, 1953; April 24, 1955; *Denver Post*, March 6, 1955; May 29, 1955; June 15, 1958.

96. *Rocky Mountain News*, September 6, 1970; September 14, 1970; *Denver Post*, September 11, 1970; Denver Dry Goods newspaper advertisement (both papers), September 14, 1970, and store-printed brochure.

97. *Rocky Mountain News*, September 12, 1971; *Denver Post*, April 4, 1971.

98. *Denver Post*, September 4, 1972; September 24, 1972.

99. Ibid., September 16, 1973; September 17, 1973.

100. Ibid., September 16, 1974.

101. Store-printed brochure, Denver Dry Goods Clipping File, Denver Public Library, Western History Collection.

102. *Rocky Mountain News*, October 9, 1982.

103. Ibid., December 25, 1958; *Denver Post*, November 23, 1955.

104. *Rocky Mountain News*, December 21, 1983.

105. F. Joseph Hayes, interview with the author, February 20, 2016; James O'Hagan, interview with the author, May 15, 2016.

Chapter 9

106. Denver Dry Goods newspaper advertisement, October 11, 1953.

107. Longstreth, *American Department Store Transformed*, 111–34.

108. The paragraphs on the Cherry Creek store are based on *Cervi's*, April 17, 1952; *Rocky Mountain News*, November 23, 1950; October 11, 1953; October 8, 1954; October 5, 1955; *Denver Post*, November 22, 1950; August 15, 1971.

109 Noel and Norgren, *Denver*, 192–93.

110. Longstreth, *American Department Store Transformed*, 170–75, 183–85.

111. *Rocky Mountain News*, August 23, 1956; August 24, 1956; *Denver Post*, March 6, 1955; Denver Dry Goods Telephone Directory, March 1, 1957.

112. The paragraphs on Cinderella City are based on *Rocky Mountain News*, March 20, 1964; November 15, 1964; July 20, 1965; *Denver Post*, May 26, 1961; November 6, 1962; November 15, 1964; March 3, 1968; March 7, 1968. Simultaneously, Von Frellick also briefly ran for the Republican nomination for Colorado governor (ending his campaign after three weeks) and then briefly for a Jefferson County district in the state senate. *Rocky Mountain News*, July 7, 1962; July 15, 1962.

113. Candelario, *Northglenn*, 7; *Rocky Mountain News*, February 4, 1968; *Denver Post*, March 13, 1968; March 14, 1968.

114. *Cervi's*, June 13, 1962; *Denver Post*, July 2, 1962.

115. *Rocky Mountain News*, April 1, 1962; February 28, 1963; *Denver Post*, September 8, 1963.

116. *Cervi's*, September 11, 1972; *Denver Post*, July 16, 1974; August 13, 1974.

117. *Rocky Mountain News*, August 14, 1975.

Chapter 10

118. Tom L. Roach, quoted in *Rocky Mountain News*, April 26, 1979.

119. This section on the wage dispute is based on *Rocky Mountain News*, November 18, 1947; *Denver Post*, July 25, 1948; August 2, 1948; August 3, 1948; August 6, 1948; August 8, 1948; December 8, 1948; February 3, 1949. The union-published leaflet is found in the Denver Dry Goods Clipping File, Denver Public Library Western History Collection. For an account of the May Company strike, see the author's *Daniels and Fisher*, 85–86.

120. *Denver Post*, December 8, 1948.

121. *Rocky Mountain News*, October 25, 1961; *Denver Post*, April 15, 1953.

122. *Cervi's*, April 17, 1952; *Denver Post*, March 26, 1949; April 15, 1953; "Denver Directions" employee newsletter, June, 1976, 5.

123. *Rocky Mountain News*, September 23, 1954; September 24, 1954; *Denver Post*, September 24, 1954; September 29, 1955.

124. *Rocky Mountain News*, March 21, 1965; *Denver Post*, March 16, 1953; March 21, 1965.

125. This section on the CORE protest is based on *Denver Post*, July 14, 1962; July 20, 1962; July 26, 1962; August 22, 1962.

126. *Rocky Mountain News*, May 21, 1961; *Denver Post*, February 5, 1972.

127. *Rocky Mountain News*, December 8, 1974; March 28, 1975; *Denver Post*, July 9, 1968.

128. *Denver Post*, September 27, 1977; *Rocky Mountain Journal*, August 27, 1975.

129. *Rocky Mountain News*, January 18, 1978; January 25, 1979; *Denver Post*, December 27, 1977.

130. *Rocky Mountain News*, April 26, 1979; February 3, 1980.

131. Hayes, interview.

Chapter 11

132. *Denver Post*, January 31, 1987.

133. Ibid., September 1, 1974; O'Hagan, interview.

134. *Rocky Mountain News*, July 27, 1979; April 3, 1980; October 5, 1982; *Denver Post*, July 12, 1973; April 8, 1974; February 4, 1975; March 2, 1977; February 24, 1978; "Downtown Denver Pedestrian Transit Mall Proposals," Denver Planning Office and Downtown Denver, Inc., 1973; "Sixteenth Street Mall Plan," C.F. Murphy Associates, 1974; "The Transitway/Mall: A Transportation Project in the Central Business District of Metropolitan Denver," I.M. Pei & Partners, Architects and Planners, 1977.

135. *Rocky Mountain News*, February 3, 1980; March 21, 1981.

136. *Rocky Mountain News*, March 27, 1986; June 7, 1986.

137. *New York Times*, July 16, 1985; *Rocky Mountain News*, June 23, 1986; July 2, 1986.

138. *Rocky Mountain News*, July 17, 1986.

139. *Denver Post*, July 17, 1986.

140. Hayes, interview.

141. *Rocky Mountain News*, February 18, 1987; February 19, 1987.
142. Ibid., February 20, 1987.
143. Ibid., March 4, 1987.
144. Ibid., February 12, 1987; March 16, 1987; April 10, 1987; May 1, 1987; *Denver Post*, January 31, 1987.
145. *Rocky Mountain News*, June 22, 1989; June 28, 1990; January 29, 1993; "Federated and May Announce Merger," press release, Federated Department Stores, Inc., February 28, 2005.

Epilogue

146. Mary Voelz Chandler, "Denver Dry Building Goes Back to Its Red-Brick Roots," *Rocky Mountain News*, December 19, 1993.
147. The epilogue is based on the following sources: *Denver Business Journal*, November 9, 1987; November 23, 1987; September 10, 1990; *Rocky Mountain News*, February 20, 1987; March 11, 1987; March 21, 1987; November 7, 1987; November 29, 1987; December 20, 1987; March 4, 1988; April 8, 1988; May 10, 1988; May 27, 1988; July 9, 1988; July 12, 1988; December 8, 1988; April 13, 1989; July 14, 1989; September 19, 1989; September 20, 1989; September 24, 1989; September 30, 1989; December 15, 1989; July 31, 1990; October 21, 1990; December 4, 1990; July 18, 1991; December 15, 1992; July 1, 1993; July 17, 1993; October 21, 1993; October 27, 1993; May 11, 1994; *Denver Post*, July 14, 1989; January 26, 1997; Rosecompanies.com, "Denver Dry Goods Building," retrieved June 5, 2016; solutions-site.org, "Downtown Redevelopment: The Denver Dry Building," retrieved June 5, 2016.
148. *New York Times*, March 28, 1993.
149. *Rocky Mountain News*, December 19, 1993.
150. *Rocky Mountain News*, October 27, 1993.

BIBLIOGRAPHY

Books

Barnhouse, Mark A. *Daniels and Fisher: Denver's Best Place to Shop*. Charleston, SC: The History Press, 2015.

Barth, Gunther. *City People: The Rise of Modern City Culture in Nineteenth-Century America*. New York: Oxford University Press, 1982.

Bird, Isabella. *A Lady's Life in the Rocky Mountains*. Sausalito, CA: Comstock Editions, 1971.

Byers, William Newton. *Encyclopedia of Biography of Colorado*. Vol. 1. Chicago: Century Publishing and Engraving Company, 1901.

Candelario, Elizabeth Moreland. *Northglenn*. Charleston, SC: Arcadia Publishing, 2013.

Hall, Frank. *History of the State of Colorado*. Vols. 3 and 4. Chicago: Blakely Printing Company, 1889, 1897.

Hendrickson, Robert. *The Grand Emporiums: The Illustrated History of America's Great Department Stores*. Briarcliff Manor, NY: Stein and Day, 1979.

Kohl, Edith Eudora. *Denver's Historic Mansions: Citadels to the Empire Builders*. Denver, CO: Sage Books, 1957.

Leavitt, Craig W., and Thomas J. Noel. *Herndon Davis: Painting Colorado History, 1901–1963*. Boulder: University Press of Colorado, 2016.

Leonard, Stephen J., and Thomas J. Noel. *Denver: Mining Camp to Metropolis*. Niwot: University Press of Colorado, 1990.

Longstreth, Richard. *The American Department Store Transformed 1920-1960*. New Haven, CT: Yale University Press, 2010.

Noel, Thomas J. *The City and the Saloon: Denver 1858–1916*. Lincoln: University of Nebraska Press, 1982.

———. *Denver Landmarks & Historic Districts: A Pictorial Guide*. Niwot: University Press of Colorado, 1996.

———. *Denver's Larimer Street*. Denver, CO: Historic Denver, 1981.

———. *Growing Through History with Colorado: The Colorado National Banks; The First 125 Years 1862–1987*. Denver: Colorado National Banks and the Colorado Studies Center, University of Colorado at Denver, 1987.

Noel, Thomas J., and Barbara S. Norgren. *Denver: The City Beautiful*. Denver, CO: Historic Denver, 1987.

Sheedy, Dennis. *The Autobiography of Dennis Sheedy*. Denver, CO: privately printed, 1922.

Vickers, W.B. *History of the City of Denver, Arapahoe County, and Colorado*. Chicago: O.L. Baskin & Company, Historical Publishers, 1880.

Zeckendorf, William, with Edward McCreary. *The Autobiography of William Zeckendorf*. New York: Holt, Rinehart and Winston, 1970.

Zimmer, Amy B. *Denver's Capitol Hill Neighborhood*. Charleston, SC: Arcadia Publishing, 2009.

Other Material

Ballenger & Richards' Seventeenth Annual Denver City Directory. Denver, CO: Ballenger & Richards, 1889.

"The Denver Directions" employee newsletter, various issues between 1976 and 1985.

Denver Dry Goods Clipping File, Denver Public Library Western History Collection.

Denver Dry Goods Company, "Report of Operations for Month of December 1923."

"The Denver Dry Goods Company and How It Grew." In "You and Your Store" employee newsletter, May 11, 1957.

Denver Dry Goods Company Downtown Store Directory, March 1957.

Denver Dry Goods Telephone Directory, March 1, 1957.

Doner, Phyllis J. "Denver's Merchant Princes: The Evolution of Denver Department Stores." Master of arts thesis, University of Colorado–Denver, 1987.

"Downtown Denver Pedestrian Transit Mall Proposals." Denver Planning Office and Downtown Denver Inc., 1973.

"Federated and May Announce Merger." Press release, Federated Department Stores Inc., February 28, 2005.

"Sixteenth Street Mall Plan." C.F. Murphy Associates, 1974.

"The Transitway/Mall: A Transportation Project in the Central Business District of Metropolitan Denver." I.M. Pei & Partners, Architects and Planners, 1977.

Newspapers

Cervi's Journal
Colorado Sun
Denver Business Journal
Denver Catholic Register
Denver Post
Denver Republican
Denver Times
New York Times
Rocky Mountain Herald
Rocky Mountain News

Websites

www.Measuringworth.com.
www.Rosecompanies.com.
www.Solutions-site.org.
www.Wikipedia.com.

INDEX